Deadwood

TV Milestones

DEADWOOD

Ina Rae Hark

TV MILESTONES SERIES

Wayne State University Press   Detroit

16 15 14 13 12   5 4 3 2 1

Library of Congress Cataloging-in-Publication Data

Hark, Ina Rae.
Deadwood / Ina Rae Hark.
p. cm. — (TV milestones)
Includes bibliographical references and index.
ISBN 978-0-8143-3449-2 (pbk. : alk. paper) — ISBN 978-0-8143-3660-1 (e-book)
1. Deadwood (Television program) I. Title.
PN1992.77.D39H38 2012
791.45'72—dc23
2011030704

∞

CONTENTS

v

ACKNOWLEDGMENTS

My family loved Westerns. The aunt who babysat me on weekends when I was five used to let me stay up past my bedtime to watch the first season of *Gunsmoke*. My father took me to see *The Searchers* at age six, and forty years later my eighty-year-old mother called regularly to share impressions of *Doctor Quinn, Medicine Woman*. In between times, we as a family watched nearly every Western television show on the air. Although they would not have made it through a minute of *Deadwood*'s obscenity, nudity, and graphic violence, I owe to them my thorough grounding in the history of the genre that precedes it.

I am grateful also to Catherine Keyser, the two anonymous readers, and series editors Barry Keith Grant and Jeanette Sloniowski for their comments on the first draft manuscript which led to revisions that strengthened it. Tracy Schoenle, my copyeditor, further improved the book through her keen eye for clarity and deep engagement with the text. Thanks also and especially to my editor at Wayne State University Press, Annie Martin, and press staffers Carrie Downes Teefey, Maya Rhodes, and Emily Nowak for making this project an enjoyable endeavor from beginning till end.

The first man who, having fenced in a
piece of land, said "This is mine," and
found people naïve enough to believe
him, that man was the true founder of
civil society. From how many crimes,
wars, and murders, from how many hor-
rors and misfortunes might not any one
have saved mankind, by pulling up the
stakes, or filling up the ditch, and crying
to his fellows: Beware of listening to this
impostor; you are undone if you once
forget that the fruits of the earth belong to
us all, and the earth itself to nobody.

   Jean-Jacques Rousseau

Original sin got us out of the garden and
got us to Manhattan.

   David Milch

When David Milch, acclaimed writer and producer for the
police dramas *Hill Street Blues* (NBC, 1981–1987) and
NYPD Blue (ABC, 1993–2005), pitched to HBO an idea for a
historical drama about cops, he intended to place the lawmen
and lawbreakers in the empire of the Caesars. As Mark Singer

notes in his 2005 *New Yorker* profile of Milch, "he wanted to write about the lives of city cops in ancient Rome during Nero's reign, before a system of justice had been codified. 'I was interested in how people improvised the structures of a society when there was no law to guide them,' he said. 'How the law developed out of the social impulse to minimize the collateral damage of the taking of revenge'" ("The Misfit").

Incredibly, the premium channel had just greenlit a series entitled *Rome* (2005–2007) that was set in the days of Julius and Augustus Caesar and centered on two everyman soldiers. Eager to close a deal with Milch, HBO executives asked if he might explore this theme in another era; he chose the American West, partly because he already had been in unsuccessful negotiations with NBC to develop a Western. The resulting series for HBO, *Deadwood* (2004–2006), premiered on March 21, 2004, and secured a renewal when initially strong ratings held up during its second week. Viewers were able to compare it with the wealth of Westerns that had preceded it on the small screen, to which it owed many of its tropes, but they also saw, for the first time on television, a show of this genre that could access the freedom of the big screen to depict violence, sexual content, and graphic, adult language. Moreover, *Deadwood* was the first television Western to debut after 9/11 and, as such, bears traces of that national trauma and its aftermath (see especially Westerfelhaus and Lacroix). All of these contributed to *Deadwood*'s singularity as a TV Western, at once traditional and unique.

Deadwood takes place in the mining camp that sprung up in the Dakota territory during the biggest gold strike in the Black Hills in the region bounded by Whitewood and Deadwood Creeks. Several attributes of this time and place created the perfect environment in which the series could explore its themes of how a civil society forms outside the many institutional constraints that characterize post-Enlightenment culture. Deadwood lay inside territory ceded to the Lakota Sioux and other Plains Indian tribes by the U.S. government in the 1868

Treaty of Fort Laramie, a treaty which included the proviso that the army keep the area free of white incursions. When gold was discovered in 1875, the influx of prospectors and subsequent Indian retaliations culminated in the massacre of General George Armstrong Custer and his Seventh Cavalry, temporarily throwing the area's status into limbo. It seemed likely that the United States would renege on the treaty, but such a step had not happened as of July 1876, the time that the action in *Deadwood* commences. Therefore, the camp lies outside any codified law or politics.

As the first season begins, Deadwood's residents are homogenous in their goals. All are there to profit from gold or to profit from trading with those who profited from gold. Naked capitalism rules the day, and the more altruistic or productive reasons that lead people to move to a new place to seek a better life are initially absent. The events that *Deadwood* dramatized during its three twelve-episode seasons recapitulate in microcosm the history of America (see Milch 12, 41) from the first arrival of European settlers and their displacement of the indigeous Native Americans to the advance of "civilization" and its attendant rules and regulations, hierarchies of government and economic hegemonies, but focus entirely on the acquisition of wealth as a motivator for those hierarchies. That a Western would so insistently concentrate on the economic basis of the settling of the frontier has been of particular interest to those who write about the series (see Worden, Salerno, Berettini, Wiggins and Holmberg).

By taking this approach, *Deadwood* dissolves several traditional binaries of the genre. While it may at first appear to set against each other individuality and social regulation, savagery and civilization, lawlessness and law, its characteristic narrative move is to demonstrate that apparent opposites are often analogues and that antagonists can morph into allies very quickly. Perhaps its biggest paradox and most profound revelation is that self-interest and communitarianism cannot survive without each other. Since the Western is so deeply imbricated in American ideology and American self-representation, *Deadwood* is quintessentially (if unflatteringly) American in what it reveals about the dark underpinnings of national success rooted not in some renewed Eden but in a town that is, in the apt words of one of its promotional taglines, "a hell of a place to make your fortune."

Lest the preceding cause *Deadwood* to sound deadly serious and unrelentingly grim, it must be noted here at the outset that it is also often uproariously funny. Indeed, the hilarious and the horrible can occur at the same moment. The second episode of the third season, "I Am Not the Fine Man You Take Me For," opens in the middle of the night as one of the camp's many roaring drunks intones the title's words, thus beginning a story now familiar to the show's viewers. All that he earned by trying his luck in the camp he lost gambling. He now owes a whore nine dollars and has no idea how he will get home. His rant is ironic in part because he stands on the platform on which candidates in Deadwood's first elections will deliver campaign speeches during the next day. As he finishes speaking, the hapless man staggers off the edge of the platform. It is a perfect slapstick moment—except that dawn reveals him still lying, dead, in the thoroughfare, the fall having broken his neck.

Welcome to *Deadwood*.

It's Not a Western . . .
It's an HBO Western

While *Deadwood* joined a long line of television Western series, its placement with HBO allowed it do things that no television Western had ever done. *Variety*'s review immediately contextualized the premiere episodes within HBO practices: "Certainly not for everyone, 'Deadwood' is nevertheless a captivating addition to the pay channel—the kind of dense, serialized and profane piece that would struggle to survive the sifting-process anywhere else and that should enthrall a passable portion of 'The Sopranos' mob" (Lowry). That network's slogan, "It's not TV, it's HBO," should not, however, weigh the scales in favor of seeing *Deadwood* as some sort of *de novo* re-invention of the genre. In some ways it merely allowed the changes that had characterized the revisionist, post-New Hollywood movie Westerns to combine with the continuing tropes of the television Westerns that flourished in the 1950s and 1960s. To understand fully how much of *Deadwood* is "TV" and how much "HBO," it is necessary to trace the state of both film and television Westerns in 2004 (the year that *Deadwood* first aired) as compared to their history from the mid-20th century on.

All genre cycles wax and wane, but for someone regularly watching network television in 1959, when Western dramas occupied slightly more than 24 percent of all programming broadcast on ABC, CBS, and NBC (Slotkin 348), it would have been as difficult to imagine a weekly schedule bereft of Westerns as it would be to imagine a weekly schedule without legal procedurals in 2011. The transformation of the Western from routine fare to noteworthy exception is most likely traceable to the intertwined cultural and social changes that occurred in the late 1960s, particularly the protests against the Vietnam War and the emergence of various rights movements and identity politics for women and racial minorities. The foundational principles of the genre—which valorized Euro-American Manifest Destiny and continental expansion, demonized the indigenous peoples it displaced, and romanticized the heroism of the asocial lone white male with a gun (who enabled civilization but never quite joined it)—could not stand their ground in the midst of such an ideological sea change. For another decade, mostly on film, the genre tried to adapt itself to this change by acknowledging the truth behind the myth, but its original themes, moved to present-day action films or making use of futuristic science fiction tropes, took over. As Richard Slotkin notes, "alternative" Westerns that served as either "formalist exercises" or "studied critiques of mainstream ideology" would relegate the genre to "the margins of the 'genre map,' and a succession of new and revamped genres have replaced it as the focus of mythographic enterprise" (633). The weight of historical culpability would never make for regular mass cultural entertainment either then or now. Although a mark of political retrenchment came with the 1980 election of U.S. President Ronald Reagan, a former actor who had often played in Westerns, the genre in both traditional and revisionist forms continued to decline. "Their failure suggests," Slotkin claims, "that the rejection of the Western had gone beyond antipathy for a particular ideology to a rejection of the very idea that the Frontier could provide the basis of a national public myth" (632).

Television had less to apologize for in regard to its portrayals of Native Americans. Although its messages of tolerance and peaceful coexistence often absolved whites in general of the nation's genocidal conduct, being happiest with "faithful Indian companions" like *The Lone Ranger's* (ABC, 1949–1957) Tonto and exemplary figures who went to Oxford or Harvard, like *Daniel Boone's* (NBC, 1964–1970) Mingo and *The Law of the Plainsman's* (NBC, 1959–1960) Marshal Sam Buckhart, it avoided the blanket racism of movie Westerns of the 1920s–1940s, primarily because television Westerns hardly existed before pro-Indian films like *Broken Arrow* (1950) had begun appearing on movie screens. (*Broken Arrow* itself came to television as a series on ABC from 1956–1960.) So the small screen didn't need to pay the penance of a *Little Big Man* (1970) or *Dances with Wolves* (1990).

As for the other main revisionist trend, the de-romanticizing of the West by showing the anti-heroism, bloodthirstiness, vulgarity, and greed dominant throughout the frontier, with very little difference between good guys and bad guys, broadcast standards by and large forbade the narrative elements that would have enabled the medium to produce equivalents of *The Wild Bunch* (1969) or *Unforgiven* (1992). Television Westerns prior to *Deadwood* therefore never went through a clear-cut revisionist period. Still, the number of Western series started to decline as the genre lost currency with post–baby boom audiences. There was a move toward genre hybrids, with the spy story in *The Wild, Wild West* (CBS, 1965–1969) or science fiction in the short-lived *The Adventures of Brisco County, Jr.* (FOX, 1993–1994) and *Firefly* (FOX, 2002). Women began to have more pivotal roles. Patriarch Ben Cartwright of *Bonanza* (NBC, 1959–1973) became matriarch Victoria Barkley in *The Big Valley* (ABC, 1965–1969). *Little House on the Prairie* (NBC, 1974–1983) may have depended on Pa to hold the family together, but the eponymous homestead was otherwise inhabited by women, and the story was told through the eyes of middle daughter Laura. *Dr. Quinn, Medicine Woman* (CBS, 1993–1998), the last bona fide broadcast network hit Western, took a full-on feminist approach with its female physician battling prejudice against her ability to practice her profession and along the way advocated late twentieth-century solutions to nineteenth-century social ills.

Revisionism of content in television Westerns, however, took a backseat to a revision in form. As the series format was fading, the miniseries Western, often running during the summer months, became a dependable staple. Beginning with NBC's *Centennial* in 1978, the genre adapted well to this shorter format, particularly in its ability to narrate epic sagas over several generations, which early miniseries successes such as *Rich Man, Poor Man* (ABC, 1976) and *Roots* (ABC, 1977) had popularized. Even well past the vogue for such miniseries, the much-watched, critically lauded *Lonesome Dove* on CBS in 1989 reminded networks of the good fit between Westerns and this format; they continue into the twenty-first century with the likes of *Into the West* (BBC/TNT, 2005), *Broken Trail* (AMC, 2005), and *Bury My Heart at Wounded Knee* (HBO, 2007). Indeed, with its 36 episodes, one could make a case for *Deadwood* as more of a very long miniseries when viewed in the context of the long-running Westerns of the 1950s and 1960s: the 268 episodes of *Wagon Train* (NBC/ABC, 1957–1965), the 430 of *Bonanza,* or 633 of *Gunsmoke* (CBS, 1955–1975), the latter of which produced more hours of programming than any other scripted drama in the history of American television.

In its content and themes, however, *Deadwood* marks the first time that the medium attempted anything like the most hard-hitting of the revisionist Western films of the 1970s and after, those Slotkin classes as "neo-realist." HBO's programming model sought to emulate the characteristics of cinema, from its industrial organization to the quality of its cinematography. The network's position within a vertically integrated multimedia conglomerate (Time-Warner) made it seem "for all the world cloned from a movie studio of the classical Hollywood era" (Miller, x). Its production values were "high—shooting on film, using long takes, filming at night, cameras on the move, single-camera production to permit multiple set-ups and loads of reaction shots as per the movies" (Miller, x). *Deadwood*'s pilot, directed by cinema veteran Walter Hill, established the series' "distinctive and highly unique" visual style: "The hideously beautiful visual referencing . . . combines a nostalgic haze with a coarse realism in its sepia tones and gritty mise-en-scène, replicating the verisimilitude of nineteenth-century photography as well as modernist interpretations of the genre" (McCabe and Akass, 88). David Drysdale notes the absence of the towering vistas and long shots characteristic of the classic Western: "Instead, the cinematography is often claustrophobic. Most scenes take place inside the cluttered camp, where there is barely room to move in the midst of crowds of people" (140).

HBO's freedom from broadcast standards and FCC oversight, the TV-MA S-V-L rating for graphic sexuality, violence, and obscene language suitable only for mature audiences, of which *Deadwood* took full advantage, allow the series to present a completely de-glamorized West that, in the opening credits, metaphorically arises from a mud puddle comprised of blood and waste as well as earth and water. Structured around shots of a horse running through various western landscapes until it passes the mining operations on the outskirts of the town, finally to stop in front of the Gem Saloon and then vanish (shown only in its reflection in the puddle), these credits intercut with the horse's progress extreme close-ups of objects that will dominate the series' preoccupations in its prevalent claustrophobic interiors: shots of whiskey, a pile of gold dust, a prostitute bathing, cards being dealt, a butcher cutting meat. Even outdoor activities find themselves fragmented as viewers see the bottom of a wagon wheel, the pan of a prospector, and the hoof of the horse itself.

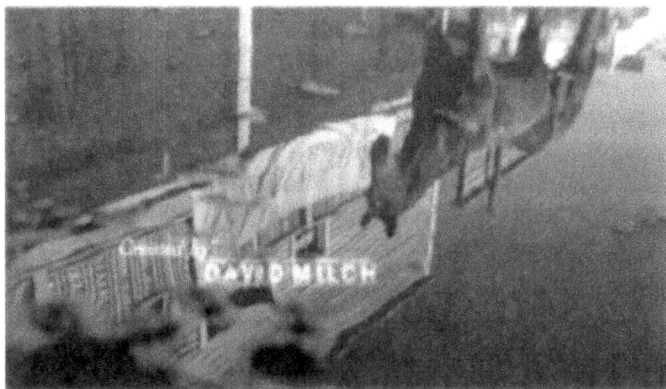

Deadwood's credits: The horse and the Gem Saloon intersect briefly before the horse fades out.

Amanda Ann Klein interprets this title sequence as follows:

> The opening credits foreground this opposition between civilization and savagery precisely because these concepts do *not* appear as oppositions within the series itself. They are, rather, the twin faces of America, past and present. Every episode of *Deadwood* opens with this "prehistory," this shorthand of the genre's central concerns, in order to further highlight the series' own deviance from the classic Western model. (99)

Milch claims to have had little previous familiarity with that model, only viewing classic Western films after completing his initial research for the series. He was struck by how far their worldview was from the history he had read, concluding that "the idea of the Western, I believe, as people conceive of it, is really an artifact of the Hays Production Code of the '20s and '30s and it has really nothing to do with the West, and much to do with the influence of middle-European Jews who had come out to Hollywood to present to America a sanitized heroic idea of what America was" (Havrilesky).

Milch's analysis neglects the influences of the dime novel and literary Western of the early twentieth century on the Hollywood paradigm and doesn't acknowledge that the 1950s were the true heyday of the genre, even if that same decade saw Westerns becoming less formulaic. But even if he was not consciously reacting against the classic paradigm in offering an America definitely not "disinfected and pure" (Havrilesky), he arrived at the same place as did many of the makers of intentionally revisionist Western films from the 1970s and after. The show's premise particularly suggests Robert Altman's *McCabe and Mrs. Miller* (1971), also a story of an entrepreneur who strikes it rich peddling drinks and prostitutes and then falls victim to larger economic interests who want to buy him out. Both even use the death of characters played by Keith Carradine as pivotal narrative moments. The only difference is that saloon owner Al Swearengen (Ian McShane) follows Mrs. Miller's pragmatic instinct for self-preservation rather than McCabe's fatally naïve and stubborn resistance. Patrick McGee, whose *From Shane to Kill Bill* reads the Western as always engaging with capitalist ideology in some way or another, praises *Deadwood* for continuing in this tradition with its "vivisection of the origin of capital and the damaging effect the war for wealth has on any kind of human relationship" (236). This evaluation echoes his reading of *McCabe and Mrs. Miller* as a Western in which "capitalism is not simply a force that exploits and threatens human beings from the outside but disintegrates the ground of their becoming, destroys the possibility of relationship or intersubjective communication, by reducing each individual to the prisonhouse of his or her own self-interests" (208).

Despite its many cinematic analogues, *Deadwood* contrasts with most HBO dramas in that it does belong to a genre with a long history on the small screen. Different as it is from *Gunsmoke* or *Bonanza*, those series do provide a medium-specific context for its differences, just as *The Wire* (2002–2008) benefits from the context of the long line of televisual police procedurals and *True Blood* (2008–) from the smaller but growing pool of vampire-supernatural dramas. By contrast, very few weekly series were set inside prisons (*Oz* [1997–2003]), Depression-era carnivals (*Carnivále* [2003–2005]), mafia families (*The Sopranos* [1999–2007]), Hollywood entourages (*Entourage* [2004–]), funeral parlors (*Six Feet Under* [2001–2005]) or polygamous families (*Big Love* [2006–2011]).

Television Westerns divide into three broad categories of place: the trail, the homestead, and the town. Trail Westerns deal with protagonists whose job or way of life is that of the archetypal peripatetic hero. He may be a hired gun or bounty hunter (*Have Gun, Will Travel* [CBS, 1957–1963], *Wanted: Dead or Alive* [CBS, 1958–1961]), or a drifter living from day to day or moving from poker game to poker game (*Sugarfoot* [ABC, 1957–1961], *Cheyenne* [ABC, 1955–1963], *Maverick* [ABC, 1957–1962]). Other trail shows give a group of regular characters a steady job that requires traveling from one point to the next, like the cattle drovers of *Rawhide* (CBS, 1959–1966) or the men who escort the covered wagons (*Wagon Train*). Homestead Westerns center on frontier families and may locate them anywhere from a modest farm to the vast land baron holdings like *Bonanza*'s Ponderosa or *High Chapparal* (NBC, 1967–1971)—which morphed into *Dallas*'s (CBS, 1978–1991) contemporary Southfork when the traditional Western faded.

Town Westerns like *Deadwood,* by contrast, focus on whole communities and the practitioners of the various occupations needed to keep them running. Most often the key professional is the town sheriff or marshal. The cinematic version of this story is the "town tamer" Western in which the newly arrived lawman must drive out or subdue the illegal profiteers who have taken over in the absence of a functioning judicial system, as in the various versions of the battle of Wyatt Earp and his brothers against the Clantons or Will Kane against Frank

Miller in *High Noon* (1952). Sometimes the criminal boss, like Jeff Surrett in *Dodge City* (1939), runs his illegal activity from a saloon that he owns (and which, Slotkin notes, has parallels with many of the Prohibition-era mobsters who work out of nightclubs in gangster films.) *Deadwood*'s first episode seems to prefigure this conventional premise underneath the amped-up violence, obscenity, and sexual content. Ex-marshal Seth Bullock (Timothy Olyphant) arrives in the camp with the intention of opening a hardware store with his partner, Sol Star (John Hawkes). Despite his desire to abandon law enforcement, however, Bullock cannot leave an injustice alone and, with the help of burnt-out former town tamer Wild Bill Hickok (Carradine), he sets out to solve the massacre of an immigrant family blamed on Indians but soon revealed to be the work of road agents in the employ of Swearengen, who has a hand in any illicit activity in the camp, in addition to his open dispensing of sex, liquor, and drugs from the Gem Saloon. When Bullock later comes to the aid of widow Alma Garret (Molly Parker), whose husband Swearengen had killed when a supposedly worthless claim he sold to Garret turned out to be one of the richest in the vicinity, it seems that the conflict between Bullock and Swearengen will anchor the series' narrative.

In *Deadwood*'s most significant thematic departure from convention, this does not turn out to be the case. By the end of the first season, Bullock and Swearengen become uneasy allies; by the end of the series, Swearengen has become the central character. As *Time*'s James Poniewozik remarks, "His greatest act of criminality was stealing the show. When *Deadwood* debuted last year, HBO did not promote Swearengen as the lead. The cast is an ensemble, and since when is the bad guy the star of a Western? But as the season unfolded, the complex, amoral yet philosophical master of the Gem Saloon came to dominate the show with greasy, foulmouthed splendor" ("So Bad"). Never abandoning a stance of self-preservation at all costs and a willingness to slit a throat or three to maintain it, the "master of the Gem Saloon" somehow also becomes the glue that holds the community together—his intelligence, pragmatism, and tactical savvy mitigating the effects of everything from plague to robber baron takeover, although many of the victories are fleeting or pyrrhic.

A community is *de rigueur* for a town Western. How much a series foregrounds the various components of that community's social, professional, and economic life can vary widely, however. *Gunsmoke* emphasized only the marshal, his comic deputies, the local doctor, and the keeper of the saloon (the latter of whom was also the marshal's discreet lover.) *Deadwood,* a serialized ensemble drama of the kind Milch had helped popularize in the 1980s and 1990s, creates dozens of recurring denizens of the town of Deadwood. There are a number of "saloon girls," notably Trixie (Paula Malcomson) and Joanie Stubbs (Kim Dickens), at the Gem and its rival, the Bella Union, respectively. Bella Union is run by Cy Tolliver (Powers Boothe), Swearengen's sometime rival. Bill Hickok's friends Calamity Jane (Robin Weigert) and Charlie Utter (Dayton Callie) hang around after his death. Prospector Whitney Ellsworth (Jim Beaver) helps Alma manage her claim. Both Al and Cy employ a retinue of hired muscle as well as bartenders, card dealers, and the like. There is a doctor, a preacher, a schoolteacher, the editor of the newspaper, the proprietor of the hotel, a telegraph operator, various storekeepers, and a blacksmith. And then there is the semi-autonomous Chinese district run by the indomitable Mr. Wu (Keone Young), whose pigs always prove handy for disposing of inconvenient corpses.

If there is one thing that the long-form television series accomplishes with its regular visits into the home, it is making viewers familiar with the characters who comprise any given program's regular and recurring cast. And this familiarity, even with characters as deeply flawed as Al Swearengen, tends not to breed contempt but affection. After all, Lt. Philip Gerard, Richard Kimble's antagonist and relentless pursuer on *The Fugi-*

tive (ABC, 1963–1967), ended up believing in his quarry's innocence and helping him prove it. On *Lost* (ABC, 2004–2010), sociopathic mass murderer Benjamin Linus switched from foe to friend of the Flight 815 survivors and managed to find redemption. Moreover, *Deadwood*'s depiction of the enforcement of the law in quirky small towns with motley groups of citizens presented to the viewer over time links *Deadwood* to such disparate shows as *Twin Peaks* (ABC, 1990–1991), *Picket Fences* (CBS, 1992–1996), *Eureka* (SyFy, 2006–) and even—hard as it is to imagine them in the same universe—to the sleepy streets of Mayberry in *The Andy Griffith Show* (CBS, 1960–1968). Because it sketches so vividly a place and the people who live and work there, *Deadwood* does what most fondly remembered series do, whether they are on a premium channel, basic cable, or a broadcast network. In this regard, it's not HBO; it's just good television.

David Milch's *Deadwood*

Announcing your plans is a good way to hear God laugh.

Al Swearengen, voicing a maxim often spoken by Milch's grandfather

Assigning authorship to televisual texts is even more difficult than in cinema. Although the place of the director as first among creative equals tips more toward the writer because of the institutional practices of television, multi-episode series employ many different writers, both on staff and as freelancers, and the makeup of the "writers' room" also changes over time. Sometimes the creator(s) of the series also guide its development; sometimes they provide the template and a few additional teleplays, but day-to-day control reverts to someone brought in by the network. The person having the most responsibility for the general direction of a television show's narrative conventions and overall plot is the showrunner. He or she may run the writers' room or just collate its efforts. Usually he or she also writes a final revision of all scripts before they go into production. Even this powerful position can rotate during the series' run, however.

On *Deadwood,* by contrast, the factors that dilute any one writer's authorship are about as close to zero as can be imagined. David Milch pitched the show, created it, wrote the pilot, and remained the showrunner throughout the three seasons. Numerous interviews and the DVD special features confirm that he rewrote every script, even though he received screen credit on only five of the 36 episodes, and frequently came to the set to explicate a scene, setting the mood and supplying subtexts and analogies from literature and philosophy in a manner that Singer describes as "intellectually daunting, digressive, arcane, wittily profane." Joseph Millichap notes that on both *Hill Street Blues* and *NYPD Blue,* "Milch came to control these productions to the point that he became their *auteur* in filmic terms, complicating the collective methodology of a television ensemble" (105). On *Deadwood* he wielded such control from the outset. Journalistic commentary on the show always led with its definition as a Milchian drama. *Variety* describes "a vulgar, gritty, at times downright nasty take on the Old West brimming with all the dark genius that series creator and writer extraordinaire David Milch has at his fingertips" (Lowry).

Thus, to begin to interpret *Deadwood,* one must take into account what David Milch brought to the table, including his life experiences, his method of working, and the exegeses he has himself provided for the series at considerable length. An academic for nine years before turning to television writing, he provides both text and a running scholarly commentary on that text. And although authorial intentions do not translate into the whole of what a televisual text delivers to its viewers, for *Deadwood* they are an imperative starting point.

Antecedent to everything was the influence and inheritance passed on to Milch from his father, Elmer, who diverged from the sometimes criminal activities of his brothers to become a renowned gastrointestinal surgeon in Buffalo. He was also, however, "multiply addicted—to alcohol, horses, and painkillers (a consequence of a near-fatal car accident two years before

David was born). He was perhaps manic-depressive, without question obsessive-compulsive, and more than capable of psychologically abusing those closest to him" (Singer). The elder Milch encouraged the young David to get involved in gambling and then berated him for his moral depravity. "That conviction of unworthiness was the deepest lesson I had been taught as a child," he told Singer, "that I was the surrogate demon who was to act and sort of expurgate the demonic in my dad. That I was to be the bad egg."

Milch replicated both his father's success, albeit as a writer rather than a doctor, and most of his personality traits. He graduated with honors from Yale and earned an MFA at the prestigious University of Iowa writing program. As both student and teacher at Yale, he attracted the mentorship of Robert Penn Warren, who told him "No one writes dialogue better than you" and compared Milch to Hemingway (Singer). His very first teleplay, "Trial by Fury" (*Hill Street Blues,* 1982), won an Emmy, a Humanitas Prize, and a Writers Guild of America award. Moreover, he accomplished all these things while addicted to alcohol, heroin, and gambling on horses, in addition to suffering from bipolar disorder and obsessive-compulsive tendencies.

During his pre-*Deadwood* career, he transmuted the gifts and demons of Milch *pere et fils* into a series of compelling, imperfect police officers played by actor Dennis Franz. Franz did double duty on *Hill Street Blues* as Detective Sal Benedetto and then as Lieutenant Norman Buntz, a character who had a short-lived spin-off show, *Beverly Hills Buntz* (NBC 1987–1988). These portrayals culminated in *NYPD Blue*'s multi-layered, flawed, but ultimately heroic Franz character, Detective Andy Sipowicz. Between the end of that series and the beginning of work on *Deadwood,* Milch finally got sober; perhaps as a result, the Milchian archetype became apportioned to several different characters in *Deadwood*—Swearengen certainly, but also Bullock and the many drug and alcohol addicts who populate the camp.

As idiosyncratic as his personality were Milch's creative processes while spinning out the narrative and speaking for the many characters in the show. Perhaps a generalized adjective for them might be "organic." Although he exhaustively researched the town's history and its denizens and incorporated a good deal of the historical record into the major plot arcs, he never had a specific plan for where the show would go from season to season or even episode to episode. Actors grew used to receiving their script pages minutes before shooting a scene and even accustomed themselves to shooting those scenes before the entire episode in which they appeared had reached the final draft stage. How Milch rewrote those drafts is described in Singer's article and is also included in a bonus feature on the season 2 DVD set. Milch would lie on the floor in the writers' trailer, facing a computer monitor, surrounded by several other staff writers and production personnel. A typist sat at the keyboard of the computer it was linked to and recorded the showrunner's dictation as he repeated speeches with subtle variations over and over until the characters had said precisely what they needed to say in precisely the way they needed to say it. (The scene being worked on for the DVD feature was a little over two pages in length and consumed five hours before Milch was satisfied with it.)

But these are the trees. From statements that Milch made before *Deadwood* premiered, throughout interviews for all three seasons, and in the definitive essay that constitutes *Stories of the Black Hills,* he seems consistently to have known the contours of the forest he meant to explore. Its topography has three main features.

1. To enforce the law, you must break the law. This is the theme that would have organized the narrative of the Roman "cop" show, the same theme that has been the central concern of Milchian television: the relationship between law, order, and violence. Because of its liminal status as Indian land likely to be taken from the Sioux but not yet reintegrated into the United

States, the Deadwood camp in the summer of 1876 is a place with "no law at all" where "warrants don't count" (1.1 "Deadwood"). This wistful assessment comes ironically from a horse thief whom Montana Marshal Bullock will hang "under color of law" as his last act in that capacity before traveling to Deadwood to open a hardware store. Although by the series' end the Dakota territory has annexed the town, and there have been local elections, most serious disputes still involve extra-legal violence. Nevertheless there is a gradual lessening of the instant gratification of killing a man in retaliation for an obscure verbal insult or the disrespecting of a woman or friend. Reparations of a nonlethal kind gradually replace the avenging of one wrong by another.

Even if achieved by violent means, order, according to Milch, is what humans in communal connection eventually seek: "Law and order are not the same thing, and tend to have little to do with one another" (Milch 119). Law lags far behind and only codifies after the fact the limits to disorder that social practice has agreed upon. For a Milch character hoping to enforce order and prevent personal retributive violence from spiraling out of control, the selective application of impersonal violence is a necessity. Statute law in *Deadwood* is either nonexistent or excercised by the corrupt politicians in Yankton, but, even in Milch's cop shows with contemporary settings, those who enforce the law can only do so by breaking it when necessary. "Cops preserve order while pretending to be interested in the law," he writes in *Stories of the Black Hills* (119). "The reason that cops only trust other cops is because they know that they've been hired to lie, they've been hired to beat the balls off people, and get them to confess so they can be excluded from society," he tells Havrilesky. "That's the first part of their job. The second part of their job is to lie about what they did. And the third part of their job is to know that if they're caught, they're going to be put in jail." If such interrogation methods occasionally surface in Milch's nineteenth-century West, what is far more evident is the way in which the camp's evolving social contract mimics the sorts of business negotiations that are the originary form of "law" in a place founded purely for the making and securing of profit from seizure by others.

An early, instructive example of negotiated violence to resolve a "legal" dispute arises with the murder of a Chinese opium courier employed by Mr. Wu and the theft of the murdered courier's cargo—opium that had been intended for Swearengen to distribute at the Gem. Wu demands that Swearengen identify the two culprits and turn them over to him for punishment. This straightforward proposal offers major difficulties for Swearengen, however. The racist whites in the camp consider consigning any white man, no matter how vile, to Chinese retributive justice an abomination. Al cannot afford to be branded a "Chink lover." On the other hand, Wu is essential to the success of many of Al's ventures, both in supplying opium and in feeding to his pigs the many corpses that Al needs to disappear when his self-interest has occasioned their murders by his hand or at his direction. Furthermore, though he would never admit it, he and Wu are friends as well as business partners.

Swearengen's first negotiation involves making Wu accept the punishment of only one of the killers. One dead white man for one dead Chinese is more than most white inhabitants of the camp would agree to; Swearengen knows that two for one is a nonstarter. His excellent deductive and interrogative skills soon elicit a terrified confession from one of his lesser minions, opium-addicted Jimmy Irons. But when Jimmy names as his accomplice his fellow addict Leon, who works for Cy Tolliver, the situation becomes even trickier. Al consults with Cy, who sneers at the idea of offering justice to a Chinese. Tactically, Swearengen realizes his only choice is to offer up Jimmy, but he stages a bogus drawing of lots between the two men, so as to send a message via Leon that he wasn't afraid to cross Tolliver if fate had so decreed. He also dispatches Jimmy himself, suddenly drowning him in his bath, before delivering the body to Wu. Although this proceeding seems hardly better than the many blood feuds that roil the camp, the fact that Swearengen essentially takes on the role of one-man, ad hoc criminal justice system (detective, judge, and executioner) mediates the pure vengeance that might occur had Wu been willing to risk hunting down and killing the two whites himself, a move that might well start a camp race war.

2. Deadwood reveals in microcosm what made America great. Since irony is one of the show's dominant discursive modes, this greatness is not the morally inflected exceptionalism of those frequently invoked narratives of a land of freedom and opportunity where success requires only honest toil. Milch specifically locates the origins of the country in a reenactment of original sin, which he broadly defines as the violation of the basic human dignity of another, whether it be stealing their goods or treating them as mere things to be exploited and discarded at will. But as the epigraph that begins this volume indicates, it is a sin that gave the nation Manhattan (Milch 46).

In Milch's view, the country became great not because of any moral superiority but because of the ways in which its citizens were able to think symbolically and abstractly, a concept that he notes as being "at the very heart of what makes us human. It's the best in us, as well as the worst, and it is often both at the same time" (Milch 55). What we do under any sign is universal, but what obtains symbolic force is decidedly local. Had the Roman cop show gone to series, that symbol would have been the cross. Deadwood operates under the sign of gold, the "universal totem" (Milch 55). The United States came into being with "the saving power of an agreed-upon abstraction . . . All men are not created equal, but we're going to accept the fiction that all men are equal. The same way that we are going to accept the fiction that gold is worth something" (Milch 55).

At its extreme, the immersion in pure abstraction, in theory, as it were, authorizes the worst atrocities that darken the true national history. Milch embodies it in George Hearst (Gerald

23

McRaney) whose exclusive passion for "the color," the abstraction that is gold, leads him to treat other human beings as "inanimate objects" (46). Viewers see him murdering any miners at his Homestead operation who attempt to organize, setting up two of his men to have their throats cut at the Gem as part of his power games with Swearengen, and partnering with a Chinese prostitution syndicate that treats the women as so disposable that it doesn't even bother to feed them. Americans watching *Deadwood* must therefore acknowledge their kinship with both Thomas Jefferson and George Hearst. As Milch concludes *Stories of the Black Hills:*

> None of us want to realize that we live in Deadwood, but all of us do. That is the point of the exercise. After first recoiling in horror, we come to love the place where we live, in all of its contradictions. To love not just America, but the world of which America is simply the most recent form of organization. American materialism, in all of its crassness and extravagance, is simply an expression of the fact that we have organized ourselves according to a more energizing principle than any civilization that came before us. (213)

In essence *Deadwood* teaches the lesson that never transcending the material makes us no different from the beasts but that going too far into an abstract view of the universe can make us forget that we—or at least everyone else—are human.

3. We are all members of one another. As a key to understanding *Deadwood* Milch frequently points to the reading from 1 Corinthians 12 that Reverend Smith (Ray McKinnon) gives at Bill Hickok's funeral. In the scripture passage, St. Paul remarks that the body of Christ has many members, just as a fleshly body does; the fact that the various members—hands, feet, head, etc.—may perceive of themselves as separate and independent does not in any way absolve them of their connec-

The avaricious George Hearst menaces Alma Garret Ellsworth.

tion as members of the same body. So Milch says to Havrilesky: "My feeling about 'Deadwood' is it's a single organism, and I think human society is the body of God, and in a lot of ways it's about the different parts of the body having a somewhat more confident sense of their identity over the course of time."

The first miners in camp, like the first "operators"—Swearengen; Dan Dority (W. Earl Brown); and Tom Nuttall (Leon Rippy), proprieter of the No. 10 saloon—come there motivated by the intense American libertarianist individualism expressed in the Revolutionary War "Don't tread on me" naval banner designed by Christopher Gadsden. Prospector Ellsworth expresses it in the colorfully obscene Deadwood idiolect when he declares to Swearengen:

> I may a' fucked my life up flatter than hammered shit, but I stand here before you today beholden to no human cocksucker. And workin' a payin' fuckin' gold claim. And not the U.S. government sayin' I'm tresspassin' or the savage fuckin' red man himself or any of these limber-dick

cocksuckers passin' themselves off as prospectors had better try and stop me. (1.1)

Nuttall later complains about new fire prevention ordinances reminding him of what he left Wilkes-Barre to escape.

It doesn't take long, however, for the residents to realize that social organization is not just about constraining individual will but also about protecting the fruits of its exercise. Well before such protections begin to be institutionalized in the camp, casual human contacts become more than that—whether friendships, romantic relationships, alliances, or enmities. There is no such thing as an untrammeled individual existence except in total isolation, and the richness of the gold strike guarantees that Deadwood will become a community whether or not its individual members desire it or initially recognize its inevitability. In delineating this community formation, Milch does have a different take than many other such narratives might utilize. He stresses that human beings connect with each other and recognize their membership in the same body less because of intention or affection than by association and action. For instance, a character may express—and indeed feel—hatred or contempt for another, but if that character's actions signal some kind of positive attachment, then mere recall of the action, or its repetition, will eventually forge such a strong connection that the initial hostile intention behind it is transmuted into fellow feeling or even love. Milch describes such a process in relation to Cy Tolliver managing to value Joanie Stubbs beyond her usefulness to him as the madam who "runs pussy" for his brothel:

> Tolliver has seen himself be kind to her, and he has seen Joanie become grateful to him. So he didn't beat her one night. Or he gave her jewelry, intending to manipulate her subsequently, and then forgetting to do it, and letting the gift stand as a gift. That action exists in the same way that a sentence exists; it has its own energy and its own life,

and it doubles back on the person who made the mistake of bringing that sucker into the world. (91)

The camp at large can see its connectedness because so much that happens starts in or spills into the crowded, fetid main thoroughfare. Swearengen spends much time out on his balcony enacting watchful surveillance, and the viewer frequently sees shots from street level of many other citizens gazing out from second floor windows. This visual trope signals a split between planning and results throughout the series. Inside, and especially in upper storeys, most of the strategizing by the movers and shakers occurs while the effects of the decisions they make manifest themselves in the crowded thoroughfare. Many episodes also foreground events that bring together much of the populace to mark ritual occasions or partake in entertaining spectacles: the funerals of Bill Hickok and young William Bullock (Josh Eriksson), the wedding celebration for Alma and Ellsworth, amateur night sponsored by the Langrishe drama troupe, Nuttall's bicycle trek.

Deadwood also literalizes the bodily metaphor that St. Paul uses. In her excellent essay on corporeality and disease in the series, Erin Hill points out its preoccupation with ailments and injuries—from headaches to plague and groin pulls to gunshot wounds—and the prominence of every possible bodily secretion or emission in everyday conversation. The dialogue's specificity of reference to the odors of a fart or a whore's vagina or visual representations of spittle, sweat, and blood are unrelenting. That every human could suffer such affliction or release such emissions stresses the fundamental similarity among those who, on the surface, might seem totally alien to each other. Furthermore, as Hill observes, "In truth, there is nothing more symbolic of community than disease, which can only be spread by people who are not isolated from one another, but rather, who are living together" (180).

Al Swearengen looks down from his balcony at the wagon bearing the murdered Whitney Ellsworth.

The show's corporeality also rubs the audience's face in the horrible intimacy of the violence that is the camp's number one communicable disease. While gunmen from a distance perpetrate many deaths and injuries, to survive in Deadwood often necessitates the willingness to kill close up. Viewers see many throats slit, stabbings to other parts of the body, savage beatings, and men's heads bashed in with rocks. Al smothers the dying Reverend Smith and drowns Jimmy Irons. One of the most gut-wrenching scenes is the protracted, no-holds-barred, hand-to-hand combat between Dority and Hearst henchman Captain Turner, which Dan wins by pulling Turner's eye from its socket and then braining him with a two-by-four. Despite being a seasoned killer, Dority finds this encounter so disturbing that he must sequester himself for many hours afterward to deal with it. Even the most bullet-ridden Peckinpah extravaganza cannot portray the searing effects of violence on the perpetrator, rather than the victim, with the immediacy that *Deadwood* can.

No one engages in such violence at close quarters more than Al Swearengen, cutthroat extraordinaire. But when he is required to kill the innocent whore Jen to appease Hearst and save the life of his former lover Trixie, he rues his failure to learn to use a gun as well as he handles a knife. In other words, this is not a killing he wants to do, and its intimacy disturbs him. Of course, he carries through anyway. He also refuses to provide Jen's beau, Johnny Burns (Sean Bridgers), with a saving fiction about Jen going peacefully. "Wants me to tell him something pretty!" Al mutters. David Milch wants his audience to value the American community that comes together in Deadwood, but he's not going to lie about the continuing violence at its core. He's not about to tell us something pretty.

Language, Decent and Otherwise

Thank you for permitting me to express myself.

Whitney Ellsworth

31

Television has always been more "talky" than the cinema, but in *Deadwood* the preeminence of dialogue approaches that of the stage. So many of its crucial scenes contain no "action" at all, consisting instead of mesmerizing conversations (or monologues). This characteristic of the series is all the more noteworthy because the Western has a reputation as the most laconic of genres "whose stock heroes . . . embody the tight-lipped, strong, silent type whose actions speak louder than words" (Benz 241). By contrast, what *Deadwood* characters confess, ruminate upon, or assert, how they construct sentences and paragraphs, what their most typical verbal responses to praise, challenge, or insult might be frequently take priority over anything they actually *do*. The energy of dialogue, as well as its frequent idiosyncrasy, often provides a comic counterbalance to the very serious matters under discussion. This was a technique brilliantly deployed by both Shakespeare and Dickens, whose rhetoric and style Milch and his writers consciously evoke.

Deadwood thus has a marked, instantly identifiable "voice," especially in light of the fact that so much television dialogue is strictly utilitarian, so that a given speech might travel from series to series to series within the same genre without ever seeming out of place. Nor is *Deadwood's* voice a mere product of its being a period piece. Every Milch program has a distinct voice. It is a trait that few of his show-running colleagues can boast of; among current writers, only Joss Whedon and Aaron Sorkin immediately come to mind as those who share Milch's gift in this regard. On *NYPD Blue* the voice sometimes became too monolithic, with all cops, regardless of differences in class, education, or race, tending to sound alike. *Deadwood* boasts a far greater range of linguistic practices and registers.

First and foremost, for most viewers, the mention of language in *Deadwood* brings to mind not literary giants but prodigious obscenity. Some early critics actually counted the number of times *fuck* or *cocksucker* occurred in an episode or a season. Milch's reasons for overloading the dialogue with swearing are germane to this discussion, but many of the other characteristics of the program's language are even more so. While a thorough survey would take up the entire length of this book, in this chapter I will examine the most significant attributes of both spoken and written expression in *Deadwood:*

1) Experiments with grammar and syntax function to give the dialogue a sound that distinguishes it from contemporary American speech.
2) The rough-hewn vernacular of the working-class, less educated characters anchors one end of a continuum that extends to the highly refined, Latinate diction of the Eastern elites.
3) The way characters use language tells the viewer much about who those characters are.
4) The difference between embodied, spoken words and those abstracted through writing illustrates the series'

major theme about the power of abstraction to transform society.

First, let's deal with that pervasive profanity. Several scholars who have investigated swearing in the nineteenth-century American West doubt that people used words like *fuck* and *cocksucker* in any but their literal sense, i.e., to describe specific sex acts, but not as all-purpose obscenities. Profanity and blasphemy instead prevailed, with copious instances of *hell, damn,* and *goddamn.* Benz speculates that Milch substituted anachronistic obscenities for these blasphemies because otherwise his characters "would not sound very threatening to modern ears" (246). It is important that these curses do carry a palpable threat, for the more violence with which a *Deadwood* character freights his or her language, the more likely it will be that this violence remains discursive and does not spill over into action. Milch also attributes his use of so much foul language to the yearning after self-determination that motivated most who came to the camp: "They wanted a liberation from the restrictions of language just as they wanted a liberation from politics" (19).

The writers deploy this swearing to good rhetorical purpose, however. When and where in a speech an obscenity falls, how often it appears, what it does to the cadence of the dialogue—all create a kind of profane poetry in the series. Consider, for example, Swearengen's recounting of the abuse he suffered at the hands of his foster father:

> I took some fuckin' beatin' after my brother's fuckin' funeral. Smacks comin' from every fuckin' angle. Still dizzy from the smack from the left, here comes a smack from the right. Brain can't bounce around fast enough. Headache I fuckin' had for three fuckin' weeks. The fuck fault is it of mine if my fuckin' brother croaks? Ain't even my

fuckin' brother. Fuckin' people take me in. I didn't ask 'em to fuckin' take me in. (2.11)

As an adjective, *fuckin'* does not necessarily imply a negative connotation. When applied to his dead foster brother and the adoptive parents who treated him badly, it certainly carries animus; one doubts that Al feels as strongly about the angle of the blow as about the man who delivered it. What the constant repetition of this one word does do, along with the staccato accumulation of sentence fragments, is to represent the blows and the pain they inflict. As expertly delivered by McShane, this monologue turns every f-word into a metonymy for the slaps and punches, and the viewer reels from them as if he or she were also on the receiving end.

34

This monologue also showcases some of the syntactic features that characterize the *Deadwood* vernacular. Subjects of sentences are often implied, so that sentences begin with the verb. Auxiliary words, as well as prepositions and conjunctions, vanish (see Benz). Inverted syntax puts the object first ("Headache I fuckin' had"). Even in the more overstuffed Victorian rhetoric of the educated speakers, the writing tends to privilege action and result over agency, to strip away "filler" parts of speech in order to emphasize nouns, verbs, and adjectives. A typical *Deadwood* vernacular locution would transform a complex sentence such as "When a man points a gun at me, he should be ready to use it" into "Points a gun at me, cocksucker better commit to using it."

The Victorian "high style" does differ from this vernacular both in terms of syntax and, especially, vocabulary. It can be eloquent and moving, as in the letter Bullock writes to the family of the murdered Cornish miner, Pasco, or an effective tool for dominating a conversation, as with Alma, who is capable of "fighting aggressively with words," using "powerful allusions, fecundity, sarcasm and irony" (Petersen 277). In the main, however, the show treats this flowery, euphemistic, and self-important language mockingly. For instance, when the newspaper editor A. W. Merrick (Jeffrey Jones) composes an urgent story about vaccinating those in camp against smallpox, he writes that the shots will be "gratis." Al wants to add "free," and when told that "free gratis" is a redundancy, insists on only "free," since few in camp will understand what gratis means. The free/gratis juxtaposition becomes a running joke in the series as shorthand for its class differences and unwillingness of the high to speak so that the low can understand.

Merrick is exhibit A for this tone deafness. His speech always sounds as if it has just been typeset, and his style—both written and spoken—is, in words he would approve of, pretentious, orotund, and platitudinous. Combined with the fact of his buffoonish appearance—heavy-set, given to plaid suits and big neckerchiefs—timidity, and hypochondria, he is hardly an endorsement for purple prose. When Merrick seeks an account of the outcome of a violent dispute between Swearengen and Bullock, he chides Al for using his normal obscene language and asks for an account that is "true and decent . . . the facts rendered fully within social standards and sensibilities." Although Al finds such a style akin to a snake swallowing its tail, he improvises a perfect parody on the spot:

> Tonight, throughout Deadwood, heads may be laid to pillow assuaged and reassured, for that purveyor for profit of everything sordid and vicious, Al Swearengen, already beaten to a fare-thee-well earlier in the day by Sheriff Bullock, has returned to the Sheriff the implements and ornaments of his office. Without the tawdry walls of Swearengen's saloon, the Gem, decent citizens may pursue with a new and jaunty freedom all aspects of Christian commerce.

Yet after Merrick leaves, Swearengen continues with a passage that betrays perhaps a longing for the Gem not to be considered so far outside the bounds of decency and social standards: "A full fair-mindedness requires us also to report that within the Gem, on Deadwood's main thoroughfare, comely whores, decently priced liquor and the squarest games of chance in the Hills remain unabatedly available at all hours, seven days a week" (2.2 "A Lie Agreed Upon, Part 2").

Swearengen can mimic Merrick so precisely because he is, as Daniel Salerno notes, "expert in all of Deadwood's discursive registers: high, low, verbal and non-verbal" (199). On the other hand, E. B. Farnum, owner of the Grand Central Hotel, has absorbed the high style's syntax and vocabulary through study but never connects organically to it, so that the disjunction between his rhetorical flourishes and his grubby, greedy, mean-spirited social-climbing nature is obvious to all. That he has not acquired a posh accent to replace his Tennessee mountain twang does not help, nor does the fact that he is easily terrified into incoherence. (Salerno [192, 200–201] provides an excellent analysis of several instances in which the high style totally fails Farnum when he is under stress.) William Sanderson, who plays him, makes the astute distinction that Farnum is smart but not intelligent (Milch 30). The lack of authenticity this distinction gives to his language, and the acquisitiveness it serves, are epitomized perfectly when he quotes Wordsworth but declares that he has never read him, a paradox explained by the fact that he has a literary digest from which he memorizes pithy phrases while suppressing all knowledge of the authors who penned the lines.

The writers also afford characters ways to reveal themselves through speech other than conversation. Timeworn theatrical devices, the soliloquy and the aside, banished from most drama since the advent of realism two centuries ago, come roaring back in *Deadwood*. Sometimes the soliloquies are addressed to a necessarily mute listener: a dog, a horse, a loved one in his grave, the severed head of an Indian in a box, a prostitute in the midst of performing fellatio. But at other times the person simply talks to him or herself. This permits the viewer to learn the motives, insecurities, fears, and aspirations of the characters without awkward expository scenes. It also allows someone like Farnum, who might otherwise be just a one-note caricature, to become incredibly richer as a character.

Farnum is a Dickensian comic grotesque whose one "humor," Milch writes, is "an obsequiousness, a need to please, which is based in an absolute resentment and a sense of inadequacy" (33). Ironically, because Farnum's insincerity and the self-serving nature of his sycophancy are so transparent, those with whom he hopes to ingratiate himself instinctively loathe him. Given all the violence endemic in the camp, he is objectively far from the most despicable resident, seeing that he never kills or seriously injures anyone. Nevertheless he is probably second only to Hearst in the contempt with which almost everyone in Deadwood views him. For some reason Swearengen tolerates Farnum, and Farnum both worships Swearengen and would betray him in a second out of greed or fear. But through the availability of soliloquy and aside, the audience sees that Farnum knows how awful he is, feels his despair at always being excluded, and marvels that this self-knowledge does nothing to ameliorate his behavior. Given to launching into a running commentary on everything that he sees—probably a desperate attempt to fashion himself as central to events rather than a despised supernumerary—he sums up his resentment perfectly when he yells across the street to where a meeting of town luminaries is taking place without him, "E. B. was left out!" Indeed, he frequently speaks about himself in the third person, as though even he views himself as object rather than subject. For instance, while on his knees trying to clean the blood of one of Al's murdered confederates from the floor, he imagines himself as Swearengen revealing how little he values Farnum's services:

The sycophantic, self-loathing sharper E. B. Farnum

Why should I reward E. B. with some small, fractional participation in the claim? Or let him even lay by a little security and source of continuing income, for his declining years? What's he ever done for me? Except let me terrify him every goddamned day of his life 'til the idea of bowel regularity is a full on fucking hope. Not to mention ordering a man killed in one of E. B.'s rooms. So every fucking free moment of his life E. B. has to spend scrubbing the bloodstains off the goddamned floor! To keep from having to lower his rates. Goddamn that motherfucker! (1.5 "The Trial of Jack McCall").

As the most skilled verbal practitioner in the camp, Swearengen also makes the best use of the ability to speak his mind to no one in particular. Whether he is commenting on Jewel's precarious ascent of the stairs carrying a breakfast tray—"Every step an adventure!"—or offering bromides to himself to calm his frayed nerves, he seemingly has to articulate his thoughts in order to build upon them. When Dan Dority overhears him talking to himself in his office, Al confides, "You have not yet reached the age, Dan, have you, where you're moved to utterance of thoughts properly kept silent? Not the odd mutter. Habitual fuckin' vocalizing of thoughts best kept to yourself" (2.8 "Childish Things").

The distinction between embodied speech and written language complements *Deadwood*'s concern with the movement of a civilization from the material to the abstract level, with the inherent benefits and drawbacks such a transformation entails. Written documents take on more and more significance as the series progresses. Merrick may seem ridiculous, but what his newspaper prints—and what it doesn't—has power. That's why his refusal to include the bureaucratically obscure announcement from Yankton about the validity of claims within the communal pages of the *Deadwood Pioneer* and his agreement to shame Hearst by printing the letter about the death of the miner whom Hearst had murdered lead to his offices being twice vandalized by the government and business interests he has defied. Hickok's letter to his wife becomes a much-prized item, and Bullock asks his spouse, Martha (Anna Gunn), to edit the text of his campaign speech. Written contracts replace the method of spitting into one's palm and shaking hands to seal a deal. Hearst is forever sending cryptic written messages to Swearengen and does much of his communication through the newly arrived telegraph.

Salerno explains Al's somewhat confounding disdain for telegraphy by pointing out that disembodied messages rob him of his formidable advantages when squaring off in face-to-face conversations (199). Yet he knows he has to be able to deal with this less material form of language and so recruits the allegiance of Merrick and the newspaperman's friend, telegraph operator Blazanov, who abandons his strict confidentiality policy and leaks the contents of Hearst's telegrams to Swearengen when the attacks upon Merrick remind him of the Tsarist thugs he fled. Moreover, Al recognizes the permanency that the written holds over the oral. When he and his colleague Silas Adams (Ti-

Wu uses pictograms and gestures to communicate with Al.

tus Welliver) work carefully to compose just the right text for the agreement by whose terms the camp will consent to become part of the Dakota territory, he forgoes a $50,000 payoff previously negotiated because it won't do to have a bribe recorded in the "founding document."

Part of the coalescence of the camp from a battlefield of warring interests to a community that is all a part of the same metaphorical body involves its inhabitants learning to communicate with each other, even if their native idiolects are as different as that of actor Jack Langrishe (Brian Cox), comforting his dying fellow thespian Chesterton by playing with him the Edgar-Gloucester scene at Dover from *King Lear,* from that of Mr. Wu getting his meaning across to Al through a combination of stick-figure drawings, emphatic gestures, and a variety of vocal inflections of the only two English words he knows: "cocksucker" and "Swed-gin."

The Social Dynamics
of Violence and Alliance

> You can't cut the throat of every cock-
> sucker whose character it would improve.
> *Al Swearengen*

Dozens of individuals weave in and out of the complex and layered plotting of *Deadwood*. Milch's *Deadwood: Stories of the Black Hills* lists thirty-five regular and recurring performers in its Dramatis Personae gallery, and that doesn't include many significant players such as livery owner Hostetler, his nemesis Steve the drunk, or telegraph operator Blazanov. Many are based on real people (Swearengen, Bullock, Star, Hickok, Jane Canary, Utter, Merrick, "Aunt" Lou, Hearst), others on fictionalized archetypes (Tolliver, Trixie, Doc Cochran, Alma Garret, Joanie Stubbs). Many of the experienced character actors who play these roles arguably give the greatest performances of their careers as Milch based character arcs in part upon what each performer brought to the table.

The majority of the cast did not bring to the table codified star images that might get in the way of viewers' responses to a character via their associations with the actors' previous roles. None of the regular cast—those billed during the opening credits sequence—had ever starred in an American prime-time television series that lasted multiple seasons (although McShane's British show *Lovejoy* [1986–1994] ran on the A&E network beginning in 1990.) A typical profile would contain many guest-starring TV roles, perhaps some supporting parts in feature motion pictures, or a regular or recurring part on a failed or limited run series, some of them produced by Milch. Welliver, for example, was a regular on *Brooklyn South* (CBS, 1997–1998); Kim Dickens was the female lead in *Big Apple* (CBS, 2001). For many of the younger members of the *Deadwood* cast, the show provided a huge career boost; Timothy Olyphant, Robin Weigert, and Garret Dillahunt (Jack McCall/Francis Wolcott) in particular were "made" by their performances in the series.

The better known names in the cast occupy roles that reflect their previous work but add a twist or another layer. McShane had done a lot of film and television in the 1980s, often playing a powerful man whose Byronic good looks made him a player in both boardrooms and bedrooms. But he had worked primarily in his native England for the fifteen years prior to *Deadwood*, *Lovejoy's* roguish antique dealer with a soft spot for those in trouble dominating his star image. Age having diminished his brooding sexuality somewhat, he was able to bring the larcenous con artist/master manipulator of his earlier roles to the less romantic and far more brutal Swearengen. Similarly, Powers Boothe used the deadly charisma and narcissism of his Emmy-winning portrayal of Jonestown's Jim Jones to inspire shudders even before Tolliver revealed his own moral rottenness. Jeffrey Jones made Merrick one of a long line of self-absorbed, pompous buffoons he had played in major motion pictures like *Amadeus* (1984), *Ferris Bueller's Day Off* (1986), and *Beetlejuice* (1988); yet Milch added strong democratic principles and a willingness to lay his life on the line for them in order to elevate Merrick beyond the stereotypical Jones characterization. Brad Dourif, who plays Doc Cochran, had begun his career with a bang by being nominated for the Best Supporting Actor Oscar for his first credited role as the mentally frail stutterer Billy Bibbit in *One Flew Over the Cuckoo's Nest* (1976). This part typed him as an oddball, either pitiable or sinister, and led him into many fantasy, horror, and science fiction projects, most notably the traitorous and creepy court advisor Grima Wormtongue in *The Lord of the Rings* trilogy (2001–2003). While Cochran's torment that derives from his failures to save wounded soldiers during the Civil War is consistent with one strain of Dourif's career, the character's humane (if cantankerous) dedication to healing his patients stands in sharp contrast to his many villainous roles.

Sanderson and guest star Gerald McRaney had the most established television personas. Sanderson had appeared in 81 episodes of the comedy *Newhart* (CBS, 1982–1990) as Larry, the only speaking member of a trio of dim-witted yet profiteering sibling handymen. His comic acumen and image as a crafty and conniving rural sharper transferred entire to E. B. Farnum, but Farnum's cowardice, self-loathing, and occasional flashes of introspection give a depth that the earlier iconic character lacked. McRaney's persona at the time of *Deadwood*'s premiere derived from his stint on *Major Dad* (CBS, 1989–1993). He played a tough-as-nails, right-wing Marine who had to adjust to the contrary views of a liberal journalist when they fell in love and he then became the stepfather to her three daughters. Playing crusty on the outside but soft in the center became the defining image of McRaney's middle years. Moreover, from the time of his first big success as one of a pair of brother detectives in *Simon and Simon* (CBS, 1981–1989), he had played men decent at the core, even if aggravating on the surface. *Deadwood*'s Hearst is a monster, yet McRaney creates a compelling portrayal without fundamentally changing his well honed performance style.

Although each creation is fully rounded and vividly detailed, this vast ensemble organizes itself around some deeper structural principles of the narrative so that similar-yet-different individuals and groupings serve to contextualize each other while simultaneously defining the norms and margins of the resident community. For instance, Cochran lost all faith in God while serving as a surgeon in the Civil War while Reverend Smith found God working in a field hospital in the same conflict. Joanie Stubbs, madam of the Bella Union saloon and later at the Chez Ami, compares notes with Alma Garret, widow of the scion of a wealthy Eastern family, about fathers who deserve a beating. Both, it turns out, were sold into sexual slavery by their fathers, who first engaged in incestuous conduct with their daughters. Joanie's may have been a farmer who pimped her out to supplement "egg money" before selling her outright to saloon keeper Tolliver while Alma's was a conniving bourgeois who maneuvered her into marrying a man she did not love in order to clear his debts, but the essential violations were identical.

Swearengen, the character who soon comes to dominate the show and diegetically authors the camp's response to the various outside forces that continually threaten its well-being, demands the most detailed analysis. His template anchors the various broad possibilities for the use of violence and participation in the social contract. Almost every character reflects a kinship with some facet of Swearengen's personality while in other respects offering a decided repudiation. A brief exchange with the Pinkerton agent, Barrett, reveals much about Swearengen's core self. Mentioning that he served in the 69th New York during the Civil War, Barrett asks "What were you doing?"

> Al: Cutting throats.
> Barrett: I was asking whose flag you were under.
> Al: The famous cocksuckers brigade.
> Barrett: Is that so?
> Al: Command of the all-whore detachment. (3.10 "A Constant Throb")

This first establishes Al's profession as killer and pimp, here given a minimum 17-year history. (By the time he establishes himself in Deadwood, he's added road agenting and swindling to his repertoire, but viewers see few instances of him engaging in the latter pursuits.) Next, the dialog tells the viewer that Al is not a man to get caught up in causes and ideologies; his only flag flies over the Republic of Swearengen. Nor does he make any bones about the first two facts. He is an unapologetic criminal who proudly never enlisted in any military unit but his own brigade. Finally, he couches the admission in his customary discourse of ironic wit and mockery—both of himself and others. To complete the picture, having disarmed Barrett with his genial repartee, Swearengen savagely kicks and beats him, tortures him for information, and finally slits his throat.

Milch contends that "Swearengen's violence is a purely pragmatic act, whether he is strangling Trixie or stabbing the road agent who worked for him" (153). This violence against Barrett turns out to be more than just that, but in the main Al does distinguish himself among his fellows as a very violent man who employs violence exclusively for utilitarian and tactical purposes and limits the occasions on which anger begets violence.

Al vents his rage against Barrett, a Pinkerton agent.

Although Milch glosses over the blows, slaps, and kicks that Swearengen visits on some of his most loyal confederates when he's not in control of a situation, the Gem boss does not ever give in to the explosive rage that leads Bullock several times to start pummeling men he despises who have made no physical move against him. As for the everyday violence spawned by the slightest insult among the perpetually inebriated "hoople-heads" who populate the camp in great numbers, Al never rises to such bait—and woe betide the man who picks a fight with him. His conversational barrages routinely fire out attacks on his hearers' intelligence, common sense, verbal tics, physical shortcomings, ethnic origins, and anything else that arouses Swearengen's frequent eye-rolling derision. Those loyal to him seem to dismiss this verbal abuse as just Al being Al; most others appear too intimidated to strike back.

The pragmatics of Swearengen's violence rests on two basic principles. The first is self-protection. If someone's continued existence threatens his safety, freedom, or profits, that person is expendable, whether friend or foe, criminal or innocent. Al even goes so far as to order a hit on the young child Sofia Metz (Bree Seanna Wall), who might link the men who butchered her family to Al, whom they worked for (even though this particular outrage was not something he had authorized). Less fatal violence is a tool to coerce or bring back into line those who have endangered his carefully planned enterprises by improvising or freelancing for their own gain. But just as he does not strike out because of anger or wounded pride, he also does not seek to hurt people simply because he enjoys it or because he cannot bear to live among people who don't cower before him, as Hearst does. Al's need to control is only a by-product of his primal fear of being controlled by others.

Secondly, violence must have short-term tactical and long-term strategic efficacy. Swearengen is far and away the shrewdest, most intelligent person in the camp. Jason Jacobs calls him "a can-do fixer who adapts to situations, but also one who can adapt environmental contingency to suit his business" (15). Sean O'Sullivan references his "hermeneutic brilliance" (123). Subordinates run to him for help interpreting or construing a complex problem. One showpiece for these skills in action is his immediate response to the Pinkertons firing on Alma (now Mrs. Ellsworth) as she walks down the street: Al barks orders to others as to how to deal with those in Alma's immediate circle as he jumps off the balcony to provide her protection, only afterward figuring out the purpose of the attack and the best way to respond to it. Less dramatic but equally impressive is the detailed proposal he puts forth at the hurriedly called meeting of camp leaders when a smallpox epidemic threatens.

These problem-solving skills combine with a gift for assessing people and gauging their intentions, which helps him decide whom he can manage with persuasion, threats, and bribes, or whom he must murder. With those who have power over him, like the territorial and federal authorities, he knows when any or all of these would prove ineffective or, worse, bring a fatal backlash against him and his interests. He will compromise and placate without pridefulness if he can see a good result down the road.

Swearengen is also tactically nimble, always willing to change plans as new intelligence surfaces or new circumstances or arrivals complicate the situation on the ground. When he receives news that Sofia has been spirited out of camp before Dan could kill her and that Hickok has shot the second of the three road agents as he did the man's brother, Al simply eliminates the surviving robber, Persimmon Phil, leaving no one alive for Sofia to identify and negating the need to silence her. And because of Milch's associational psychology, deciding to spare the life of a child, even out of expediency, "begins to generate other neural pathways in your brain. When you see the child you like her, because you remember that you were kind to her" (153).

Many new neural pathways must have fired up in Al Swearengen's brain to get him from the man viewers meet in the first episode to the man he is at the end of the series. In the Shakespearean register that marks much of his dialogue, especially his frequent soliloquies and asides, our first impression is of Richard the Third, but upon longer acquaintance, viewers get a glimpse of Hamlet, complete with Yorick's skull in the form of "Chief," the severed head of an Indian brought to him for a bounty. (Salerno prefers Iago and Falstaff as Al's Shakespearean analogues, [197] but I think he lacks Falstaff's *joie de vivre* and excessive appetites.) In the Dickensian register that informs much of the stylized characterization, his public face combines, according to Jacobs, aspects of Bill Sikes and of Fagin (21), but viewers learn that in his past he was more akin to Oliver Twist. As his character arc culminates, Al, all-seeing on his balcony, has become father, son, and unholy spirit, the one Deadwood's citizens turn to in their hours of need because the deity whose presence Reverend Smith's brain tumor deprives him of never seems to intervene in the camp's far too earthly affairs. If repeated metaphors that render Swearengen a Christ figure don't make this clear enough, in "Sold Under Sin" (1.12) the scene of Cochran's prayer to God and Christ to end the minister's suffering directly precedes Al's mercy killing of him, which ends with the benediction "You go now, brother."

McShane's charismatic, dominating performance led the series to re-center itself around Swearengen after the first season. Still, he is a bit of a hard sell as "the series' unquestioned hero" (Klein 99) after all the murders he commits or orders committed for his own personal gain and after his brutal treatment of Trixie—the boot to her throat and the painful "snatch grab" that propels her toward a suicide attempt. Therefore the second season begins by having Al undergo one of the "body crises" that Hill correctly identifies as making possible "rapid character evolution on *Deadwood,* each season of which takes place over an extremely compressed period of time" (174).

The crisis comes in two parts. Swearengen, dismayed that Bullock is so "cuntstruck" in his illicit passion for Alma as to be

useless as the respectable front Al needs in the battle to have
Deadwood annexed to America on the most favorable terms,
calls Bullock out about it in the street. When Seth doesn't see
reason but rather challenges Al to a fight to avenge his and
Alma's honor, Al suffers broken ribs and a badly bruised and
swollen face. In a preview of events to come, he returns to Bullock the badge and gun Bullock left in the Gem, publicly hu-
miliating himself for the good of the camp, saying:

> I offer these and I hope you'll wear them a good long
> fucking time in this fucking camp, whosoever's fucking
> thumb we're under. And where it come to me just a few
> moments ago that the Reverend Smith—may he rest his
> soul, he was found on the road, apparently murdered by
> heathens just some months ago—what he said on the
> subject of you, "Mr. Bullock raises a camp up, and I hope
> he'll reside with us and improve our general fucking at-
> mosphere for a good long fucking time, even with all the
> personal complications and fucking disasters that we all
> fucking have, and where running away solves absolutely
> fucking nothing." (2.2)

Of course, it would not be Al talking if he did not at the same
time brazenly invoke the name of Reverend Smith—whom he,
not Indians, killed—and provide counsel on Bullock's domestic
entanglements.

Even as he sustains injuries in fighting Bullock, Swearengen has begun to suffer the symptoms of the body crisis that
almost takes his life. Kidney stones have obstructed his ability
to pass urine. The stones cause excruciating pain; growing sep-
sis renders him unable to move and deprives him of a weapon
only slightly less lethal than his knife, his voice. In "Requiem
for a Gleet" (2.4), the only episode of *Deadwood* in which Al
Swearengen speaks not one word, harrowing depictions of his
struggle to pass the stone with the agonizing assistance of Doc

Cochran's instruments inserted into his penis alternate with testimonials of his closest associates' devotion to him.

Temporarily suffering the debilitating effects of a mild stroke as well, Swearengen begins to experience empathy for and identification with those he formerly ridiculed, abused, or exploited. Jewel, who has cerebral palsy, notes that he now drags his leg like she does. Under siege by Hearst, he can relate to how Chief must have felt when the white man was intent on taking his land. When the compliant whore Dolly—who performs fellatio on him according to a strict and hectoring regimen that Swearengen articulates during the act—agrees with his hatred of being held down, he realizes, "I guess I do that, with your fucking hair."

Even as Swearengen begins to see himself through the eyes of others, the audience receives information about his origins that allows them to fabricate an exculpatory biography through which to rationalize his skewed interpersonal relationships (although the character always retains enough ambiguity to deny him any excuses). In the famed "blow-job" monologues, Al ruminates upon his childhood while Dolly services him. Viewers learn that he was the son of a whore who abandoned him at an orphanage run by a pimp, a place to which he returns to buy the Gem's whores in a twisted combination of exploitation and rescue. Then a family adopted him, only to have the father constantly beat him out of grief for a biological son who had died of epilepsy. It is not much of a leap to conclude that this background would produce a man who cannot imagine loving or being loved and who would work to create emotional barriers between himself and others through verbal abuse, intimidation, and proclamations of self-interest as his only motivator. During the fight with Bullock, Swearengen stops dead upon seeing young William, just arrived on the stagecoach. "Cow-eyed kid looking from that coach—that's what fuckin' unmanned me," he explains (2.1 "A Lie Agreed Upon," Part 1). Remembering his own vulnerability as a cow-eyed kid transforms him from the cold-blooded murderer he became to his former cowed and fearful self.

From the very beginning, Swearengen reserves his deepest fear and contempt for the Pinkerton agency. He makes his decision to have Brom Garret suffer a fatal "accident" only when Garret threatens him with Pinkerton intervention. Thus, when Pinkerton spy Miss Isringhausen offers Al $50,000 to sign a false affidavit pinning the murder on Alma, he instead goes straight to her with the information, explaining that "I don't like the Pinkertons. They're muscle for the bosses, as if the bosses ain't got enough edge," although implying that it also serves his self-interest: "Bein' the Hearst combine and their fucking ilk got their eyes on taking over here, your staying suits my purpose. . . . those are my prejudices and personal interests for siding with you. Also . . . if you want to match their 50, that'd be between you and your God" (2.7 "E. B. Was Left Out"). It takes a little while longer for him to realize that he, too, is one of the bosses in the small pool that is Deadwood and to admit to a more communitarian hatred of bullies, regardless of one's own financial or class interests. Thus, when Al visits his wrath upon Barrett, he admits to acting on behalf of others. "So you'd shoot at a fucking woman?" he shouts. "Beat that poor newspaper bastard? Scare that Chinese with your fucking horses?" Most of his schemes during the second and third seasons serve the community at large. Milch describes Swearengen as "a very good man with none of the behaviors of goodness" (17) but in writing him, he does find it necessary to ameliorate the badness of the bad behavior as the series progresses.

Hatred of bullies animates Swearengen's seeming antagonist but actually perfect complement, Seth Bullock. Alma's father, the abusive and manipulative Otis Russell, profiles Bullock precisely: "Were you bullied, Mr. Bullock, when young and incapable? Now you see wrongs everywhere and bullying you feel called to remedy?" This explains how Bullock gravitates toward positions as a lawman. But he often cannot contain the explosive rage he feels whenever confronted by injustice. Swearengen doesn't embark upon violence unless he's considered all his options and then only when he can carry out violence hidden from public view and with plausible deniability does he take action. But Bullock can go off like a rocket at the slightest provocation, sometimes at ancillary targets if the real cause of his anger is unavailable, and often in public. Swearengen calls him a maniac and chides his lack of self-control. After Russell's remarks quoted above, Bullock soon is beating him within an inch of his life in the middle of the Bella Union saloon. Similarly, he almost kills Farnum when he only suspects that E. B. might have told Hearst about Seth's affair with Alma Garret. On the trail to bring Jack McCall to justice for shooting Hickok after the unofficial Deadwood court finds him not guilty, Bullock is attacked at close quarters by an Indian. He just manages to prevail in the intense hand-to-hand combat but is not content to render his assailant unconscious or even dead. "I wind up after, beatin' him till I couldn't recognize his face," he confesses tearfully to Sol. "For Christ's sake. That Indian saved Jack McCall's life, I'll tell you that fuckin' much" (1.7 "Bullock Returns to the Camp").

It is for good reason then that Bullock doubts his fitness to be a lawman and is running away from such an obligation to start over in Deadwood, where there is no law to enforce, as an ill-suited hardware merchant. But he is drawn to justice like a moth to a flame. When Tolliver's lackey, Con Stapleton, declares himself sheriff and connives with his confederate, Leon, to kill an innocent Chinese man, Bullock snatches the badge from his coat and throws it down in the mud. Then the moralistic General Crook, who is passing through to re-provision after engaging with the Sioux, advises him that "in a camp where the sheriff can be bought for bacon grease, a man, a former marshal, who understands the danger of his own temperament, he might consider serving his fellows." Bullock finally approaches Swearengen to take him up on the suggestion, previously refused, to put on the badge and become "the fuckin' sheriff" (1.12). As Milch observes, "He is going to disinfect his own murderous rage through the law" (121).

"Disinfect" is a telling word choice here. In order to rein in his passions, Bullock has to have access to a rigid and somewhat sterile code of behavior. The series provides a key to what this implies as it portrays numerous occasions on which Bullock insists on carrying through with proper funerary rites. When executing the Montana horse thief, he makes sure that someone will see that the body receives proper burial and the prisoner's last wishes be conveyed to his sister. He contributes to the death of Ned Mason, too, but also attends his funeral. When he realizes that the Indian he fought to the death attacked him for intruding on his burial of a murdered friend, he learns from Charlie Utter the proper way to arrange the man's remains according to Native American custom. The penalty he levies on a prankster who caused another man to be shot for an insult he perpetrated is to see to the unfortunate victim's burial. He complains about the disrespect of having Hickok's remains displayed. Viewers also learn that when his brother died in Mexico, he traveled there to bring the body home.

Everything that is emotionally alive in Seth Bullock is so wild and dangerous that he must, essentially, lay it to rest in the most respectful manner possible. This plays out in his romantic life as well. The affair with Alma is out of control and reckless, and the only way that Seth can imagine their having a chance together is to abandon the community and leave behind her adopted child, Sofia. Alma can't accept those terms and breaks it off with him, leaving him to find some way of living with his wife and former sister-in-law, Martha, whom he married only out of duty. It is perhaps not so accidental, at least symbolically, that her son, William, and the unborn child he and Alma conceive both die. There is something anti-life about Seth Bullock that makes it impossible for him to be a father even as his willingness to sublimate his life force in bringing order to the community makes him its worthy steward. From this paradox, perhaps, derives the great irony that no event so unifies all the citizens of Deadwood as William Bullock's funeral.

The third prominent attitude toward committing violence characterizes George Hearst, who emerges in seasons 2 and 3 as the true villain of the series. At first glance, as a man who consolidates power and preserves it by disposing violently of any opposing him, he seems merely a Swearengen who has the financial clout to employ the very deadly and professional Pinkertons rather than Dan Dorty and whatever ragtag marauders are available for hire. But early on Al notices a difference:

> Pain-in-the-balls Hearst. Running his holdings like a despot, I grant, has a fucking logic. It's the way I fucking run mine. It's the way I'd run my home if I fucking had one. But there's no practical need for him to run the fucking camp. That's out of scale. It's out of proportion, and it's a warped, unnatural impulse, this fucking cocksucker! (3.1 "Tell Your God to Ready for Blood")

The warped, unnatural impulse is sadism. "Were you whipped, Mr. Swearengen?" Hearst taunts. "And does the lash snap still? Do you wait for the strike after all these years?" Al answers with the speculation, "Would the grip have been the part you were versed with?" (3.2). As Hearst makes clear in several different contexts, he is not satisfied until all people and all institutions "bend to my will." When Swearengen refuses and instead answers him with his usual defiant sarcasm, Hearst has his men hold Al down while he cuts off his middle finger with a mining tool. This symbolic castration coincides with Hearst knocking out the wall of his room opposite the Gem and standing on its roof, an assertion of his intention to usurp Swearengen's ever-present gaze upon the camp. His need for absolute control goes so far beyond any pragmatic reasoning that he's the one antagonist whom Swearengen completely gives up trying to figure out.

Hearst on occasion torments even those who don't defy him, as in a stomach-churning scene in which he spits twice on the cowed Farnum's face (having already bought his prized hotel out from under him) and threatens him with death should he ever wipe the spittle off. Hearst has no compunction about hiring Tolliver as his front man in the camp, even though he (correctly) considers Tolliver "a lying, blackmailing sack of shit." Hearst then offers his terms of employment and their perverse rationale:

> Your duties will be to answer like a dog when I call. . . . Complications of intention on your part in dealings with me or duplicity or indirection—behavior, in short, which displeases me—will bring you a smack on the snout. When administered by a practiced hand such a blow can be more painful and grievous even than your recent sufferings. . . . My proper traffic is with the earth. In my dealings with people, I ought solely have to do with niggers and whites who obey me like dogs. (3.3 "True Colors")

To this Cy replies, "If he hadn't meant me to wag it, sir, why would the Lord give me a tail?" (Swearengen, by contrast, laughs at the idea of Hearst renewing friendly overtures after amputating his finger, as if he expected Al to be like a beaten dog who would still return to its master for a scratch behind the ears.)

Even though Tolliver finds his true place as Hearst's cur, he shares his sadistic impulses, displayed when two young grifters try to rob him; he tortures them while forcing Joanie and faro dealer Eddie Sawyer, who have grown fond of the two, to watch. When he arrives on the scene in the third episode of the first season, "Reconnoitering the Rim," he appears to be the serious rival to Swearengen that only Hearst truly turns out to be. Cy may have an upscale place that need not cater to the

Gem customers who "don't wash" but he doesn't have the legitimacy and class status to enforce his will. Nor does he have Swearengen's accurate criminal instincts. When he attempts to bribe or blackmail, Tolliver invariably targets precisely the wrong people (General Crook, Hearst) who turn the tables on him with ease. All he can really do well is be a panderer, in all senses. An unstable foundation of degeneracy, cowardice, and disloyalty underlies all his enterprises and relationships. Whatever one thinks of Swearengen, he is rock solid in his "fierce matter-of-factness. He was who he was, unadulterated" (Milch 12). Tolliver, by contrast, always seems fundamentally rotten at his core, his identity maintained by constant improvisation and always threatening to fall apart in a fit of hysteria.

The Bella Union itself serves as a metonymy for Tolliver. Elegant and lavish in its appointments and boasting finely clothed prostitutes, it exists primarily to defraud. All the games of chance are rigged, and the employees are mostly cardsharps and conmen. (Whatever violence and criminality it fronts for, viewers never hear that the Gem waters its drinks or cheats its gamblers.) In such an atmosphere of exploitation and distrust, community does not have a chance. When longtime associate Andy Cramed shows up at the Bella Union while ill with smallpox, Cy panics and has him left to die in the woods. After the incident with the young grifters, Eddie Sawyer robs Cy and gives the money to Joanie so that she can escape his financial hold on her. Found and nursed back to health by Calamity Jane, Cramed returns to camp and stabs Cy when Cy ridicules his conversion to the ministry. Of the two associates who stick by Tolliver the longest, Leon is a viciously racist opium addict, and the aptly named Con Stapleton is a venal buffoon. And in the last episode of the series, Cy, furious that Hearst's reward for his good-dog groveling is only to make Cy "his fucking quartermaster," stabs Leon to death in a fit of pique.

The lesson here is that even the most beaten down cur will eventually turn. All who subordinate themselves to Hearst end

The finery of the Bella Union saloon disguises the rottenness in Cy Tolliver's soul. (Also pictured are Leon and Janine.)

up wanting to kill him just as much as do those he oppresses. Cy brandishes a gun at the tycoon's departing stagecoach. The cook Lou Marchbanks, Hearst's former slave and current employee, plays the stereotypical Mammy fawning over the master to his face but mutters under her breath, "Kill you if I could, George Hearst." Even that most groveling of sycophants, Farnum, finally does wipe the saliva from his face and vow, "I'm going to fuck you up!" Men like Hearst may efficiently amass wealth, but they destroy community and trust. Their violence solves no problems and rights no wrongs but simply propagates just as virulently as do the quarrels and revenge-taking among the hooples.

Although the writers fudge a bit on the whys of it, Swearengen's sometimes abusive conduct toward his subordinates neither drives them away nor makes them want to kill him. None of them plots to take over his enterprises when he is gravely ill but instead swap stories about how much worse off they would be without him. "A creature walking 'round on hind legs. Just like Crop Ear and them half-dozen bushwhackers out in the forest, ones I'd fall in with or out—whatever suited my daily purpose," says Dority. "That's what I was till I crossed paths with Al" (2.4). Even the fickle, greedy Farnum is more hesitant to betray Swearengen than anyone else: "Loyalty expanded is not loyalty betrayed. I contemplate no disloyalty to Al Swearengen. I feel exposed. I don't like being weak, and I know that I am. I yearn to rely on a stronger will. I fear what I'm capable of in its absence" (2.4). Trixie counters Jane's contempt for Al because he threatened Sofia's life with the assertion that Al took Jewel from the orphanage and gave her a job cooking and cleaning at the Gem because "it's his sick, fucking way of protectin' her" (2.3 "New Money").

With the caveat that his adopted family's dynamics are conducted in a "sick, fucking way," it's clear that Swearengen functions as a father to those he employs at the Gem. Silas Adams, Dan Dority, and Johnny Burns (whom I always think of as the wise, wicked, and simple sons from the Passover service) constantly behave as brothers engaged in a vigorous sibling rivalry for his approval. Dan is even reduced to tears when Al takes Adams's side in a dispute. Given the stern, disciplinary role assigned to fathers in the Victorian era, Swearengen is perhaps not so far off the mark as he would appear to twenty-first-century eyes. He counsels self-improvement by relentlessly pointing out faults yet protects his "children" from the dangers that unwise actions might entail. This protection extends to allies as well. He has both Ellsworth and Wu kidnapped and restrained when he knows that they are about to act on impulse against Hearst's forces and risk being killed; he excludes Farnum from the meeting about Charlie Utter's beating of Francis Wolcott because he knows that if Farnum became privy to the facts revealed there, "blackmail would have proved irresistible, and pursuin' it would have gotten you murdered" (2.7).

Yet neither master-slave nor sick patriarch-child dynamics can provide the paradigm for a healthy community. That possibility arises from *Deadwood*'s Bullock nexus. Despite the sheriff's tendency to erupt into violence, his own relationship to power involves a network of colleagues and confidants on whom he relies to constrain his worst impulses. Despising tyrants, he doesn't seek subordinates. He treats Sol Star as his equal partner in the Star and Bullock hardware store and in fact defers to his superior acumen as a businessman. Charlie Utter tried, unsuccessfully, to anchor Hickok in the same way and becomes a natural choice to act as Bullock's deputy. Indeed, Hickok passes the torch to Bullock by attaching himself to him upon their near simultaneous arrival in Deadwood. He gives him a "cowboy" nickname, Montana, no doubt as someone once dubbed James Butler Hickok "Wild Bill." As Douglas Howard writes, the nation now needs "men like Bullock, as opposed to Hickok, to protect its people, to carry out its laws, and to preserve its order" (51).

As both lawmen and small businessmen, Bullock and Utter, the latter of whom starts up a freight office, represent legitimate financial interests, those who can thrive without murder being one of the tools of the trade or women used as consumer goods. Although the complex issue of *Deadwood*'s portrayal of sex and gender power dynamics is the subject of a subsequent chapter, it is worth noting here that one salient characteristic across the Bullock nexus is the capacity of its male members to serve as nature's gentlemen when women are in distress. Bullock married his wife, Martha, because she was his brother's widow, left alone with a son to raise, and he begins his involvement with Alma as a commission from Hickok to ascertain the value of her claim and act as her agent. Ellsworth, who is appointed to manage the claim, agrees to a marriage of convenience with Alma when she becomes pregnant with Bullock's child. Charlie becomes Joanie Stubbs's protector after she leaves the Bella Union and even delivers a Bullock-style beatdown on sexual psychopath Francis Wolcott when Charlie learns that the man has murdered three women working in Joanie's own bordello, the Chez Ami. Sol manages to give the volatile Trixie an alterna-

Seth Bullock and his wife, Martha, host his deputy, Charlie Utter, and business partner, Sol Star, for supper.

tive to her life as a whore, becoming her lover gratis and training her in bookkeeping.

Yet Trixie remains loyal to Swearengen and still acts as his agent, as do other more natural fits with the Bullock nexus such as Merrick, Blazanov, and Cochran (not to mention, reluctantly, Bullock himself). Al knows that his own skills can go only so far in protecting the camp, that a showdown solely between his gang and Hearst's Pinkertons would end up with Deadwood erased from history and only forest grown back in its place. Because he recruits, protects, and advises those like Bullock who are "those pains in the balls who [think] that the law can be honest," he can devise a solution that avoids Armageddon yet imparts the cutthroat savvy that the legitimate citizens lack.

Deadwood essentially tells the story of how this union among pragmatic self-interest, a hatred of those who abuse power, and a belief in justice births a community that stands in for the nation's best instincts while acknowledging that its contest with the nation's worst can at best only result in a draw.

Deadwood's Political
Economic Narrative

> We, who have pursued our destiny out-
> side law or statute, will be restored to the
> bosom of the nation.
>
> *A. W. Merrick*

For the past 25 years, the narrative structure of each episodic television drama has fallen somewhere on a continuum between having each installment tell a self-contained story, so that the occasional viewer is never at a disadvantage when dipping in or out of a program's first run or is catching it in reruns, or telling one continuous story from first episode to last. The networks, still dependent on revenue from advertisers who want their commercials viewed live at the time of broadcast, have usually insisted on at least one self-contained story per episode, even if longer story arcs are part of the total picture. The success of one heavily serialized program is enough to spawn several more before the inevitable retreat to police procedurals or medical dramas with discrete cases to be solved within each episode.

Compromises that have worked well for the Big Four (ABC, CBS, FOX, NBC) could point to *The Fugitive* as a template.

Overall, Dr. Richard Kimble fled pursuit by Lt. Philip Gerard to return him to the death house (i.e., the term given to death row in the show's opening narration) while he himself sought the "one-armed man" who had actually killed his wife. Several episodes per season might focus on this *über*-plot, but each week Kimble also moved on to a different location and became involved in the personal dilemmas of strangers that he helped ameliorate.

Cable channels, especially after the advent of DVDs and online viewing, could more readily risk serialized storytelling in which the individual episodes might begin and end *in medias res*. Many HBO dramas are thoroughly serialized, and *Deadwood* is no exception. Since the heyday of the Western generally preceded the tilt toward serialization, this marks another way in which *Deadwood* stands out from other examples of the genre. That events occur over a very short period of time helps make its serialization work. Each season spans less than a month. A title in the pilot reveals that, after a brief prelude, viewers first see Deadwood in July 1876. The elections that conclude the series are held in November 1877. There is a seven-month gap between seasons 1 and 2, and there are six weeks between seasons 2 and 3. The rationale behind having the action occur only in the summers or autumns of the two years probably has to do with the difficulty of portraying a snowbound Dakota winter while filming on location in Santa Clarita, California, just north of Los Angeles.

This is not to say that *Deadwood* is all one long story containing no discrete subunits. The various health crises have their beginnings, middles, and ends. For instance, the smallpox epidemic begins when Cramed becomes symptomatic and ends when the vaccine arrives and all those infected previously have either died or recovered. Many guest stars become recurring characters, but some have a story that plays out over just a few episodes, like the grifters Miles and Flora, who are introduced and dispatched within two hours of showtime. An appearance by Wyatt and Morgan Earp in season 3 is also of short duration, but their somewhat comic portrayal does not fit organically into the grim struggle with Hearst that surrounds it. Similarly, although historical personage Jack Langrishe works well to expand our view of Swearengen, since the two are old friends and relate as equals—a situation hitherto unseen with Al—the various subplots concerning his acting troupe have rudimentary development and also don't complement the larger events of the story.

Even the most episodic of shows allow the characters to change and grow, and often love relationships provide a catalyst for these arcs. Alma anchors the dominant romantic plot in *Deadwood,* a tragic one that sees her first and second husbands murdered and her passionate affair with Bullock ended. More happy results ensue as Sol becomes Trixie's lover and Joanie begins an intimate relationship with Jane.

Nevertheless *Deadwood* does not foreground personal stories as a broadly defined soap opera might, nor does it derive its overall arc from a mystery or conspiracy plot, such as *The X-Files* (FOX, 1993–2002) or *Lost* (ABC, 2004–2010). History shapes its overriding narrative; politics and economics unify its thematics. Although the writers take considerable liberties with precise historical details, especially in regard to biography and chronology, most of its tentpole events really happened: the smallpox outbreak; annexation and the protests over the first appointed officials, which resulted in elections; and the Hearst organization consolidating mining operations in the Black Hills. The speculation by newspaper editor Merrick from which this chapter takes its epigraph in essence announces in the very first episode what the series' master narrative will be. History and gold, politics and economics become interchangeable terms in charting it. His speech begins: "Paradoxes, the massacre at Little Big Horn signaled the Indians' death throes, Mr. Utter. History has overtaken the treaty which gave them this land. Well, the gold we found has overtaken it. I believe

63

within a year, Congress will rescind the Fort Laramie Treaty; Deadwood and these hills will be annexed to the Dakota Territory." Though politics and economics are deeply intertwined in the series, this chapter examines politics first and then the economics that always shadows it.

Much as the hooples proclaim their libertarian hopes that Deadwood remain under no larger hegemony than that of the individual, the more astute residents know that this situation is unsustainable. Should the Indians somehow regain the rights granted under the treaty, the U.S. Army would either drive the whites out or withdraw its protection, leaving the community open to violent reprisals by those they have dispossessed. Given the amount of wealth the Hills produce, that possibility is a very remote one, even before the slaughter of Custer's Seventh Cavalry provides an excuse for the American government to abrogate the Fort Laramie Treaty. Since annexation is thus inevitable, the first two seasons of *Deadwood* deal with the camp positioning itself to be annexed on terms most favorable to its interests. Secondarily, members of the camp contemplate the changes that individuals may undergo as they create or renew their identities as Americans.

The first conundrum to present itself concerns how the community can establish its own governance without seeming to proclaim itself a sovereign entity that the United States might treat as more deserving of a hostile takeover than a welcoming embrace. This issue surfaces early in season 1 when the community decides to try Jack McCall for shooting Hickok in cold blood. Had someone in the No. 10 immediately gunned down McCall in response, all would have been well. But setting up a legal proceeding is dangerous, as Swearengen tells Tolliver:

> We're illegal. Our whole goal is to get annexed to the United fuckin' States. We start holdin' trials, what's to keep the United States fuckin' Congress from sayin', "Oh, excuse us, we didn't realize you were a fuckin' sovereign

community and nation out there. Where's your cocksuck-ers' flag? Where's your fuckin' navy or the like? Maybe when we make our treaty with the Sioux we should treat you people like renegade fuckin' Indians. Deny your fuckin' gold and property claims. And hand everything over instead to our ne'er-do-well cousins and brothers-in-law." (1.5)

Indeed, Swearengen sees any punishment of McCall under the color of a nonexistent law in Deadwood as so inimical to his and the camp's interests—because of stirring up "the vipers in the big nest in Washington"—that he tells Magistrate Claggett, the presiding judge, that he has had a "vision" of his men kill-ing McCall rather than letting that happen; however, a far better solution, which he hints at and Claggett acts upon, is for the judge to charge the jury in a way that ensures acquittal.

Yet there are times when communal well-being requires some sort of political organization, as becomes clear when the epidemic strikes. Swearengen essentially puts on the mantle of community organizer when he selects those he thinks most able to deal with the threat and contribute the funds needed to obtain the vaccine. He well knows that he is not the sort who could ever be elected to public office or admitted to the halls of power through the front door. But he is also a skilled political operator of the kind who still populates the back rooms and lobbying ranks. So when Claggett informs him that "the pres-ence of an *ad hoc* municipal organization . . . would enable the legislature to say Deadwood exists, we don't have to create it," Al once again charges the "city fathers" to "be in my joint in two hours. We're forming a fucking government." He later amends the charge to stress that it cannot be officially a government "but structure enough to persuade those territorial cocksuckers in Yankton that we're worthy enough to pay them their fucking bribes" (1.9 "No Other Sons or Daughters").

The shooting of these two meetings in episodes six and nine of the first season emphasizes the evolution from a one-time assemblage of individuals to an ongoing community administration. In "Plague," shots that include everyone at the table are minimal. The extreme close-ups that are *Deadwood*'s trademark dominate, with occasional two-shots providing variety. Shadowy sepia tones prevail; the bright sunshine, seen through the windows, seems unable to penetrate. Only at the end of the sequence, after Reverend Smith has suffered a seizure and there is a shot from his point of view, looking up at the men gathered around him, do viewers get a sense of the group united in a common endeavor. The second meeting features a larger table; as more men consider themselves community leaders, they don't sit as close together, and there are more shots of the whole group or at least four or five at a time. The light is still diffuse but brighter and whiter. Although "Plague" has a generally more claustrophobic visual style overall than "No More Sons or Daughters," in part because of the contrasting techniques of directors Davis Guggenheim and Ed Bianchi, the differences complement the transition from truly "ad hoc" to ongoing (if "temporary") governance.

That the "municipal organization" formed is still merely a sham, however, becomes apparent when the official positions are filled with self-nominations by people totally unsuited to each task: Utter as fire inspector, Bullock as health commissioner, and, most egregiously, Farnum as mayor. Independent of charades to placate Yankton, Deadwood is most in need of a sheriff, an office not up for grabs at the meeting. The essential political plot arc of the first season takes Bullock from giving up his badge in Montana to pinning it on again in Deadwood. He does so in a room in which the blood from Claggett's slit throat still stains the floor.

Because bribing Yankton has not secured the promised results, the effort to win annexation on favorable terms shifts to different methods and occupies the political plot for the second

The camp leaders attend to the Reverend Smith after he has a seizure. (*Clockwise from top center:* Tolliver, Dority, Nuttall, Burns, Cochran, Swearengen, Farnum, Star, Merrick.)

season. Using Star and Bullock's local knowledge, Swearengen and Adams con the foppish, craven, and despicable Commissioner Hugo Jarry, appointed by Yankton to govern the county to which Deadwood has arbitrarily been assigned, into believing that Montana is also interested in making a bid for annexing the camp. The ruse succeeds, and Al predicts (correctly): "We knocked the cocksucker up. And soon he will find himself deliverin'. . . elections" (2.10 "Advances, None Miraculous"). Jarry comes to represent all that Deadwood the community and *Deadwood* the television series find reprehensible in politicians. In the third season he reveals himself even more fully; he demonstrates his willingness to prostrate himself before power and wealth when he falls to his knees before an incredulous Hearst, offering to be Alcibiades to his Socrates. The most decisive put-down comes from Wolcott, the sexual psychopath, who remarks after a brief conversation with Jarry: "I am a sinner who does not expect forgiveness. But I am not a government official" (2.10).

The season 2 finale, "Boy-the-Earth-Talks-To," marks the high point in the course of the series concerning Deadwood's political ascendancy. Its many intertwined plots pivot on the question of new alliances moving forward while old problems recede. Three events or event clusters come to a conclusion on this day/episode. First, Alma Garret weds Ellsworth so as to give the baby she conceived with Bullock legitimacy. As a corollary, Bullock and his wife try to carry on as a couple despite William's death. Second, Yankton has agreed to terms on guaranteeing elections in return for Deadwood committing itself to be part of the Dakota territory. Third, Hearst arrives and reviews the status of the agents who have been working on his behalf. He withdraws his connection with Wolcott upon learning of the murder of the Chez Ami prostitutes; agrees to consider Wu as his representative among the camp's Chinese, should Wu "prove out" in competition with the current Hearst Chinese ally, Lee; buys the Grand Central Hotel (while keeping Farnum on as manager); and rebuffs Tolliver's crude blackmail attempt.

The central metaphor here compares the wedding and its subsequent revelry, accompanied by music and dancing in the main thoroughfare, to the coming together of the citizenry under the banner of American democracy. The episode intercuts the marriage vows with the approval and signing of the annexation agreement by Swearengen, Jarry, and Bullock. Merrick interrupts the dancing by passing around a special issue of the *Deadwood Pioneer* carrying the headline that the territorial governor has agreed to elections. At the same time, anti-communal forces are expelled. Wolcott, devastated by his rejection, hangs himself from the balcony of the livery stable. Cramed "guts"— but does not kill—Tolliver. Both unification and expulsion coalesce in Wu's takedown of Lee. The often fractious Swearengen "sons," Dority, Burns, and Adams, team up with the Wu to slit the throats of "the San Francisco cocksucker" and his henchmen, returning in triumph like a latter-day Three Musketeers and D'Artagnan. Wu then looks up to Al on the balcony and uses the knife that dispatched Lee to cut off his queue, holding the blade and the braid in hand and proclaiming, "Wu! America!" Al acknowledges that these two actions, using violence to stake one's claim and severing ties with old allegiances and customs, initiate Wu into full citizenship: "That'll hold you tight to her tit." Finally Wu declares a more personal bond, crossing his index and middle fingers and gesturing toward Swearengen with the exclamation "hang dai" (brother), which Al returns.

Keone Young, who plays Wu, says on the DVD special feature that cutting off the queue, which he suggested to Milch, demonstrates that to become fully American, the immigrant must first "deface" the old identity. Since everyone in the camp has symbolically left and then returned to America, this principle applies universally. Swearengen's amputated finger might be read as an extreme example of it. A less drastic way that *Deadwood* enacts such defacements occurs when characters don unfamiliar and not totally appropriate dress. For the wedding celebration Ellsworth struggles with having to wear kid gloves—or "mittens," as he calls them—because the effete, cosmopolitan tailor insists that they are a fashion must. Meanwhile Joanie prevails upon Jane to put on pantaloons and a dress. In other episodes, Utter frets that the frock coat he has adopted for the grand opening of his freight business does not suit him, and Farnum, upon declaring himself mayor, abandons the threadbare jacket and trousers he has been wearing in favor of a series of pastel silk suits and ruffled shirtfronts. Even the deviant Wolcott feels a pull of sartorial uncertainty when he asks if his hat makes his head look big. (A close-up of this hat beneath the shadow of his hanged body is the last that viewers see of him.) Wu himself returns from a trip to San Francisco to recruit Chinese mine workers attired in a ridiculous-looking pinstriped suit and bowler.

These transformations don't point so much to America requiring a conformity of appearance and behavior but rather to the capacity to reach beyond insular, parochial identities and

69

alliances. For instance, as the second season begins, Johnny Burns cannot understand why Swearengen would reach out to Bullock, who is not among Al's "flock" of trusted confederates. Dan Dority replies: "Al's gonna be calling numbers to the fold now that he can't trust like us. Some he don't even like. We're joining America. And it's full of lying, thieving cocksuckers that you can't trust at all—governors, commissioners and what not. By God, that's just the new way of things" (2.1). The members of the polity that assemble to dance after the wedding have learned to trust one another at least a little, even if they dance different steps to the same tune: Ellsworth performs a jig with Sofia; Blazanov demonstrates the Cossack crouching kick; Jane, Joanie, and Charlie square dance; and Cochran and Jewel reprise the waltz they first performed to try out her new leg brace.

Al had watched that first dance from the interior balcony of the Gem, and that's where he stands, accompanied by the box containing Chief, as the rest of the town comes together. Like the classic Western hero, he enables community without ever joining it. Here he at least begins to tap his foot to the music as the episode closes. Another such moment occurs in "Amateur Night" (3.9) when Swearengen does not attend the performances but, as he is alone wiping the bar at the Gem, sings to himself "The Unfortunate Rake," an earlier version of the ballad that became "The Streets of Laredo." During the first event to bring much of the town together, William Bullock's funeral, Al again banishes himself while allowing his whores to attend. Having shown private anguish while the boy's life was ebbing away, he also strains to observe the ceremony from his exterior balcony but hastily runs inside when his employees return, lest they realize his interest. Milch observes that "Swearengen believes he is in solitude, but in fact he is absolutely engaged with the world" (17). Likely this belief stems from Al's certainty that to be known to feel for others makes one vulnerable; at any rate, his seeming aloofness in these situations keeps him

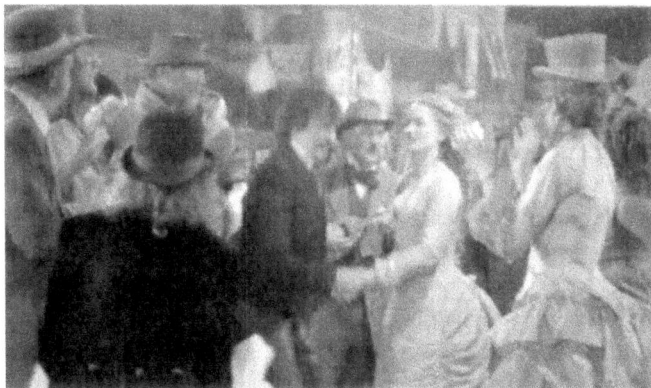

Sol and Trixie take their turn at the street dance that brings the community together after Alma marries Ellsworth.

from ever fully integrating into the town that, the show suggests, could not survive his absence.

For obvious reasons Bullock does not join in the wedding festivities, although he does linger at the Gem until he can exchange a glance with Alma before she departs on her honeymoon; Bullock then turns for home, urged on by Al. Bullock's rigidity and explosive temper isolate him also from full communal integration. The ability to deface oneself and emerge into a new American identity is very difficult for him. "What I've done, Sol, and you have to admire me for it," he confides wryly to his partner, "is moved 300 miles to set the same situation up I left Montana to get away from" (1.10). But even the unaltered identity comprises a violent opposition. "Are you a cunt-driven near maniac or a stalwart driven by principle? The many cannot tell, for you yourself are so fucking confused," Swearengen berates Bullock in "Childish Things" (2.8). Bullock can at least have these contradictions softened and domesticated at work by Sol and at home by Martha. While he thus does not have to choose only to voice his self-doubt to the decapitated head of an Indian, he still is too volatile to fashion any dance to the fiddler's tune.

Nevertheless, Deadwood is at this moment as unified and contented as it ever gets, a moment whose duration is brief. Like the union of Alma and Ellsworth, the democratic alliance of Deadwood with Yankton is a mere marriage of convenience. As the series' last season proceeds, both of these break down under the unrelenting "abstraction" of George Hearst's obsession with "the color." Both the first season's arc of Bullock being destined to become sheriff and the second season's arc of Deadwood finding a way to have a voice in its political destiny get overturned when Hearst's amalgamation and capital buy the elections and oust Bullock from the office of sheriff.

> If money had to be clean before it was re-circulated, we'd still be living in fucking caves.
>
> *Sol Star*

In one of the most astute readings of the series yet produced, Daniel Worden posits that "*Deadwood* remakes the western into a prismatic account of life within neo-liberalism," which he defines as "the set of economic and political policies designed to foster free markets and limit governmental controls over finance capital" (223). Yet, he adds, neoliberalism at the same time paradoxically demonstrates that individualized neoliberal subjects "who exist in a free market environment, unregulated by state controls and genteel codes of behaviour . . . have the potential to form strategic alliances that break the very logic of the free market from within. By acting as self-interested agents, individual neo-liberal actors can form collectives that place limits on the free market" (235). Probably the most singular characteristic of how these collectives function on the show regards "the fact that it does not seek to recuperate bourgeois values.

Even when advocating for decency or public institutions such as prisons and schools, Deadwood's residents do so only at the intersection of individual interest and collective responsibility" (Worden 241). As Star responds when Bullock expresses surprise that Swearengen has sprung into action to deal with the smallpox epidemic: "The dead don't drink or chase women must be his thinkin' on that subject" (1.7).

If the vicissitudes of Seth Bullock's career as reluctant lawman organize the arc of a collectively sanctioned communal authority, then the history of the Garret gold strike at claim nine above Discovery organizes the free market plot. (Both begin in the first episode and conclude in the last.) The original claim holder, Tim Driscoll, deeply in debt at the Gem, agrees to dangle what all believe to be a worthless claim in front of newly arrived dude Brom Garret. Al is orchestrating the scam with Farnum posing as a competing bidder; Farnum will be paid a flat fee after Al gets 70 percent of whatever Garret pays while Driscoll will receive 30 percent. Brom comes from money and is holding "a full faith letter of credit for $20,000 from the Bank of New York" that his family has staked him to for his Deadwood adventure. While not the typical prospector looking for the first significant payday of his life, Brom does wish to prove his worth independent of his inheritance and can be counted as another neoliberal subject.

Everything sorts out according to plan when Garret buys the claim for $14,000. But Driscoll gets greedy and sets out on his own to reopen the bidding and take Garret all the way to his total stake of $20,000. Not only does upping the price risk his backing out, but, as Swearengen later explains, since Garret will now have to wire home for more money, his family will start sniffing around and may send in the Pinkertons. Acting in his own self interest, Al has Tim killed for disobedience, and later, when Brom, after having second thoughts, overtly threatens to bring in the Pinkertons if he doesn't get his money back, Al has him murdered also.

73

Here are revealed the inherent flaws in both untrammeled free market individualism and government intervention in the economy as *Deadwood* conceives of them. Business is impossible with just one participant, yet any contingent alliances formed for mutual gain can collapse when one of the parties seizes upon an opportunity that benefits that person individually but works to the detriment of the others. Conversely, any entrenched institutions of aggregated capital become indistinguishable from a regulatory governmental hand in their powers to constrain individual self-interest. Much of what follows the first few episodes of course demonstrates that actual government is a wholly owned subsidiary of entrenched capital. Indeed, Farnum asserts, "More than providing services to them, taking people's money is what makes organizations real, be they formal, informal or temporary" (1.9 "No Other Sons or Daughters"). Worst of all, without some sort of collective understanding of how the neoliberal community is to operate, violence is the first recourse in resolving conflicts.

The function of the Garret claim alters radically when it turns out not to be a worthless property used by conmen to swindle a naïve, wealthy Easterner for a sum far in excess of its value. On closer examination, it proves to be a rich find now owned by his laudanum-addicted widow. Swearengen and his agents therefore reverse themselves and attempt to buy back the property before Alma realizes its worth. Swearengen even sends Trixie, on the pretext of caring for Sofia, to addict Alma to unadulterated opium, thus making her more compliant. But Alma marries her self-interest to a collective expertise. She reaches out to Hickok, then Bullock, who in turn brings in Ellsworth to evaluate and later oversee the claim. Trixie, at much personal peril, helps Alma kick her drug habit rather than compounding it. This collaboration with others ultimately serves the widow's economic interest, assuring her that she is in possession of great wealth that it would be foolish to trade away for what it had originally cost. She then reciprocates by using her fortune to put up capital for the Bank of Deadwood, the first local financial institution.

Once Swearengen hears that the Sioux and Cheyenne have made peace and annexation looms, he gives up his efforts to obtain the Garret claim. The riches to be gained via favorable terms from Yankton make Bullock as respectable front man essential, so Al must forego his usual recourse to murder when negotiations fail, as he confides to Farnum in "Suffer the Little Children" (1.8). When he suggests to Bullock that the camp needs to make some noises about perhaps forming its own territory or even becoming a "republic," in order to persuade Yankton to offer some inducements if Deadwood is to join Dakota, the sheriff is surprised that Swearengen would not find dictatorship his preferred form of government. "What the fuck do we need a dictatorship for, that silences the public voice, that eases the enemy's way?" Al retorts. "Noise made, overtures to outside interests and enlistment of the hooples' participation is what this situation demands" (2.8).

This is, to be sure, rank hypocrisy, in that Al feels he has every right to act as "despot" to his underlings but has no use for any form of government that might exercise such control over him. Yet the fact that communal democracy may preserve his individual tyranny makes him the camp's leading advocate of free elections, even when they don't turn out his way. Milch has said that if the series had gone forward, he would have dramatized the historical aftermath of Bullock's defeat by Harry Manning (Brent Sexton), which was that Bullock refused to recognize the validity of the election and barricaded himself at his ranch, unwilling to surrender his badge and gun or the keys to the jail. The real Bullock finally stood down when he was served a court order, but Milch was going to have Swearengen persuade him because Al "understands that this act of submission has to take place . . . It's a submission of the self to the democratic process" (149).

Ironically, though, the strong-arm methods and con artistry that Swearengen abandons in favor of manipulating the political process resurface in the community with the arrival of Hearst's advance man, Wolcott. Deadwood's fate as a part of the United States hinges on one pivotal point: whether property claims will be honored, since none of them have been codified by law. Hearst's plan is to exploit this uncertainty in order to entice nervous claim holders to sell at a discount, out of fear of being left with nothing. He first uses Farnum to spread rumors that claims will be nullified and then sets up Tolliver as a front for the Hearst interests, providing him with all the cash necessary to buy from any who are willing to sell. Later these fears gain credence when Jarry publishes a notice that although U.S. law grants title to those who have continuously occupied and improved property, since Deadwood was not a part of the U.S. when these claims were established, "This presumption shall be subject to qualification according to mitigating facts. New title will be awarded on claims to which title is denied at set prices via lottery. As conducted by the County Commissioner" (2.5 "Complications"). The notice so outrages the hooples that they mob Jarry as he cowers behind the cashier's cage at the Bella Union. Tolliver, true to form in throwing allies to the wolves at the slightest sign of trouble, does nothing to forestall the mob, leaving it to Bullock to restore order.

Even as the community celebrates its democratic empowerment through elections at the end of season 2, much individual control over economic destiny has already been lost. In a letter that Wolcott sends to Hearst in the eighth episode of season 2, he predicts the time when "workers at wage outnumber individual prospectors in the camp," a situation that will permit the importation of cheap Chinese laborers to enable 24-hour mining operations. More importantly, "with purchase of the claim formerly operated by the Manuel brothers, we will control save one—the Garret property—every considerable deposit now discovered." The final season thus focuses on Alma's ultimately futile struggle to retain control of her claim. Her naïve proposal of collaboration, with her giving up 49 percent share of her claim in exchange for 5 percent of Hearst's Deadwood holdings, enrages him so much that he nearly rapes her in retaliation. After Hearst's campaign of intimidation against her climaxes with Ellsworth's murder, she capitulates.

Vesting Bullock with the power to enforce order and turning to politics to gain advantage had limited the use of violence as a tool of free market economics, but with Hearst everything comes full circle. He represents the worst neoliberal nightmare: a ruthless business competitor backed by the regulatory power of government rather than constrained by it. He freely confesses that he cannot bear residing among other people and feels right only when alone in the wilderness listening to the earth whisper to him of the color. Since the elections might empower Bullock to constrain him, he simply buys the votes to defeat him, having formerly proclaimed that if elections don't further his will, he "neuters" them.

As Hearst returns the camp to its more primitive days in which cutthroat competition was literal, the Swearengen group must return to its old ways. Dority kills Captain Turner. Al slits Barrett's throat where once he watched Adams slit Claggett's. (Johnny notices that it's been almost a year since they had to change the rug in Al's office, which is a record.) And once again Trixie shoots a brutal man. The dialogue underscores the parallels. When she kills an abusive john in the first episode, Al exclaims, "Loopy cunt!"; when he hears that she has shot Hearst, he says, "Loopy fuckin' cunt." This has all been presaged earlier, when Mose Manuel reenacts the biblical first murder, shooting his brother because he'd rather hold onto their claim than surrender it for disenfranchising riches.

At the end of season 3, in the series finale, Hearst finally leaves Deadwood to seek after copper in Montana. The murdered prostitute Jen has been offered up to him, like the sacrifice of a (not so) virgin to appease the angry god of the volcano.

The town still stands, and characters will no longer have to fear Hearst's capricious acts of sadism. Yet he leaves with a firm grip on the camp. He has consolidated all mining operations under his oppressive hegemony, turning the place into a virtual company town peopled by wage slaves rather than independent entrepreneurs. His Pinkertons remain, in an uneasy standoff with Swearengen's marauders and Wu's Chinese troops, all standing in the background as Hearst's coach gallops away. In a parting shot, Hearst informs Merrick that he has established a rival newspaper to hew to his own editorial line. Milch writes that "Swearengen's violence puts limits on Hearst's violence and lends strength to the emerging order" (151). But it's hard to see much triumph at this point, except what is derived from the community still surviving, though subject to a tyrant's will.

Women and Power

> Guess if you've got a pussy, even owning a
> bank don't get you to that table.
>
> *Jen*

I n the season 1 DVD Special Features, Milch points out that in 1876 the Deadwood population was 90 percent male; of that 10 percent who were women, nine out of ten were prostitutes. The show de-romanticizes the "saloon girl" archetype to show its sordid reality: abuse, venereal disease, multiple abortions, drug addiction, suicide. It is therefore no surprise that female empowerment is a very small part of *Deadwood*'s story; however, the symbolic uses to which the whores' plight are put raise the question of how sincere the writers are in critiquing this sad state of affairs. Rather, they appear to exploit it in the service of telling stories sympathetic to men.

The insistent obscenity and the many scenes set in whorehouses create a sexually laden atmosphere for *Deadwood*. Such scenes and obscenity also frequently serve to crystallize the fears of those men who came to the camp to seek their fortunes. Many of them, failures elsewhere, hope that in this land with no law they will achieve economic self-sufficiency and with it the secure sense of manhood that their pasts have in various ways called into question. To compare a rival male to a woman (or a homosexual) who is on the receiving end of male sexual dominance is a standard ploy in masculinist rhetoric. Of the many humiliations that drive Jack McCall to shoot Hickok, surely the oft-cited speech in which Wild Bill compares every feature of the man to a "cunt" ranks near the top. Similarly, Charlie Utter uses the slur to explain his intuition that it's safe to beat up Wolcott (played, like McCall, by Garret Dillahunt) since the dangerous serial killer only makes helpless women his victims: "But I am good at first impressions, and you are a fucking cunt! And I doubt you've fought many men, maybe even one!" (2.7)

Swearengen specifically extends metaphors of a man being treated as men treat the "pussy" he trades in at the Gem to describe the fate of the camp as a whole if it does not resist total control by Yankton and by Hearst. "Our moment permits interest in one question only: will we, of Deadwood, be more than targets for ass-fucking?" he says. "To not grab ankle is to declare yourself interested. What's your posture, Bullock?" (2.8). But there is a disconnect in that Al sees "ass-fucking" as unnatural only if it happens to men. He does not connect the impulses that lead him and his customers into the systematic degradation of women as symptomatic of the very behaviors that characterize the powerful interests he aims to resist. In fact, the first two avatars of Hearst who arrive, Wolcott and Lee, are, respectively, a psychopath who slits the throats and mutilates the genitals of women and a pimp who starves his sex slaves and then throws their bodies into bonfires as if they were no more than kindling. Hearst's own equation between intact manhood and complete control, especially over a woman, reveals itself when Alma offers to make him a minority partner in her claim:

> Hearst: A vulgar man would ask before proceeding any further if you would require him to produce his jackknife and make himself a capon before you.

Alma: What in my ideas do you find emasculating?
Hearst: I can offer no inside explanations, Mrs. Ellsworth,
 as I am not a capon, which details offend me and why
 your proposal offends completely. It mistakes my nature absolutely. (3.3)

Deadwood thus makes the point that the fate of most men under
unregulated capitalism is analogous to that of women under patriarchy, especially patriarchy in its most brutal form: prostitution. But does the series avoid finding only the former perverse
while, like Al, naturalizing the latter?

Milch writes, "Bought sex is a grim business that is always
disrupted by an awkward truth: The women are human." But
he muddies the waters with his second point: "In Deadwood,
that humanity keeps asserting itself—in the women, of course,
but also in the men" (81). While one of *Deadwood*'s glories is
how it allows every character his or her humanity, viewing
them in the round and allowing them to make their cases, no
matter how vile or foolish they are, there is not a moral equiva-
lence between the man who finally realizes that the woman he
has victimized and objectified is a human being and the woman
herself. In his commentaries, Milch relies overly on the "beauty
and the beast" sort of myth in which a sinful man's love for or
being loved by a woman redeems him.

This is especially true when Milch talks about the two
pimps, Swearengen and Tolliver. He repeatedly asserts that by
recruiting his whores from the very orphanage to which his
mother abandoned him, Al both exploits and rescues them.
One really has to wonder what sort of hellhole that orphanage was for life as a Gem prostitute to qualify as rescue. Both
Milch and McShane assert that Al truly loves Trixie—so much
so, Milch writes, that "at a certain point, Al conspires to get
Trixie to fall in love with someone else, because he wants her to
be happy" (90). This does indeed describe the way Swearengen
pushes her to stay in the relationship with Sol when she pan-

81

ics and wants to return to her familiar identiy as "Trixie the Whore." Nevertheless, to stress Al's identity as self-sacrificing matchmaker obscures the brutality that he displays in the early episodes of the show toward this woman he supposedly loves. Even more astonishing are Milch's comments about Tolliver and Joanie. Unlike Swearengen, Tolliver undergoes no discernible moral evolution during *Deadwood*'s three seasons. He is still vicious and corrupt in general and stalker-ish and controlling toward Joanie. Although she acknowledges that she owes him for support without which she would have probably ended up dead, she still calls him "devil incarnate" and refuses him entry to the Chez Ami as if he were a vampire looking for an invitation to come in and suck her blood. Yet Milch remarks that if the show had gone on longer, "Tolliver, who is the most oppressive person in the world, will wind up becoming, over the course of five seasons, the great philanthropist and feminist of Deadwood" (91). (I have to say that I would crown Milch the greatest television writer in history had he been able to bring off such a transformation convincingly.) Kim Akass has questioned whether soft-pedaling Swearengen's misogyny might reflect anxieties about women in *Deadwood*'s creators, and many of Milch's statements do nothing to contradict such a conclusion.

Since Milch's statements aren't on the screen, however, this chapter investigates the depiction of *Deadwood*'s women that is. Just as it would not be fair to judge the men by the behavior of the average hoople, so viewers shouldn't judge the women by the actions of the semi-anonymous prostitutes shown lounging around the Gem and the Bella Union. Featured female characters do have all the vividness and complexity of their male counterparts. Five play major roles in the series: Jane Canary, Joanie Stubbs, Trixie, Alma Garret Ellsworth, and Martha Bullock. The latter four play variations on the classic Western paradigms of the sexually promiscuous "whore with a heart of gold" and the prim and proper lady from the East; Jane is the outlier, opting instead to assume the gender attributes of a man. Before examining these characters individually, it is prudent to discern some similarities.

All except Martha fall short of the Victorian ideal of womanhood, but the others have internalized this ideal to the extent that they seem filled with self-loathing for falling short of it. Jane adores Sofia but feels herself too bad an influence to remain her caregiver. Trixie has trouble thinking of herself as anything other than a whore and is bemused and terrified that Sol "stares in my eyes when he fucks me, longing-like" (2.6 "Something Very Expensive"). Joanie cannot get over the guilt of having allowed her father to corrupt her sisters as he did her. Alma complains of Doc Cochran's judgmental attitude toward her as a shorthand for defensiveness about both her opium addiction and her affair and unwed pregnancy.

Nor is Alma the only one to have turned to substance abuse to alleviate her emotional distress and the constraints placed on women of the era. Trixie has kicked an opium habit but chain smokes as a substitute. Jane is an alcoholic. Joanie, although sober, has strong inclinations toward self-harm: "If I could, I'd tear my skin off. If I could, I'd put out my eyes," she tells Utter. "Cy knew what I was. He knew to pick me all those years back" (3.2).

Given the psychic toll exacted by their transgressions of gender norms, it's no surprise that the character arcs for these women tend to pull them toward the Victorian ideal. Jane is, of course, the farthest from it, but much of her transvestism proves more apparent than real, despite her success at masculine occupations such as army scout and mule skinner and her proud account of being courted by a young Finnish man who, after gifts of flowers and dried fish, declared, "I want to suck your cock." Played overwhelmingly for comedy, her assumed masculinity is the worst kind on display, a parody of the typical hoople behavior. She is perpetually drunk, foulmouthed, pugnacious. Her usual banter is of the "bust your balls" variety as she subjects even those who are most fond of her to strings of insults. "Hardware Jew at less than full force, now they'll be fucking quaking," she says sarcastically as an injured Sol arrives on the scene to back up Seth's face-off with Al over the return of his guns. And she tells the hefty Mose Manuel, loyal protector of her and Joanie, that she thought he was "Giganto, the runaway circus elephant." Only Bill is exempt. Jane worships him unconditionally, mostly because he has always accepted her unconditionally for who she is.

Yet Jane's true nature emerges as much more stereotypically female than her outward behavior would indicate. She can be intimidated by men like Swearengen and Tolliver. She is a skilled nurse, bringing the sick and injured back to health when they might well have died under someone else's care. And she loves to tend children, even if feeling herself too drunk and profane for the privilege. The series finds for her the perfect blending of her masculine and feminine tendencies as she becomes Joanie's lover and the two of them serve as assistants to Martha Bullock in the Deadwood schoolhouse.

Trixie also rebuffs gestures of affection with a profane, combative front, often going off at people for very little reason because her history has not prepared her to trust much besides her own instincts. Her instincts are savvy, however, and one of her signature behaviors involves her working out a strategy in her head and then trying to communicate it to others while in the middle of her own thought processes, so that the listener has only a hazy idea of what she's talking about. A prime example occurs when she is proposing to Ellsworth that he marry Alma Garret so as to provide cover for her pregnancy; Ellsworth wonders if she thinks he fathered the child, and their back and forth generates considerable humor for the viewer before Ellsworth understands. As Petersen notes, Trixie's language "is oftentimes elliptical, meandering through her meaning. The words themselves have little import—instead the way in which she speaks them creates an impressionistic cloud that conveys her intent" (277).

Jane Canary and Joanie Stubbs walk the camp's children to their new schoolhouse.

Trixie progresses throughout the series from abused whore to fledgling bookkeeper loved by a good man. But the path takes many twists and turns given her own changeable nature. Trixie often defies an oppressive man and at the next moment either re-submits to his authority or falls into suicidal despair. She shoots and wounds Hearst after he has Ellsworth killed but immediately thereafter is begging Sol to kill her. She wants to get away from Swearengen and yet returns to him time and again. She does finally come to grips with why she behaves this way, telling Sol in one of her most lucid speeches: "Now, hold to this counter as I reveal this, Mr. Star. I've lived most of my life a whore, and as much as he's her misery, the pimp's a whore's familiar, so the sudden strange or violent draws her to him. Not that I wouldn't learn another way" (2.11 "The Whores Can Come").

Although Joanie has committed multiple transgressions of the socially sanctioned sexual norm for proper Victorian ladies (prostitute, madam, lesbian, incest survivor), she resembles Alma Garret more than she does Trixie. She dresses beautifully, is clean and well coiffed, and eschews profanity for a refined speech that is more forthright than the convoluted evasions of the Eastern upper classes but a far cry from the Deadwood vernacular. Indeed, of all the women, she sounds the most like a contemporary of the viewer. More significantly, like Alma, whose plot arc has already been discussed at length, she frees herself from male domination and sets up her own business, only to have it all collapse in a bloodbath.

Petersen, viewing *Deadwood* through a feminist lens, sees the final disposition of its women characters as a warning for what can happen to contemporary women's progress when confronted with a post-feminist backlash: "Just as the women of Deadwood begin to stretch out in their newly found freedoms, society, embodied by Hearst, effectively puts them back in their 'places' as submissive, dependent, disposable accessories" (279). Female independence and aspirations to power don't survive in *Deadwood*—although the same is true of many men in the show once the Hearst juggernaut rolls into town; however, Jane, Trixie, and Joanie end up happier and less oppressed, all three in loving relationships, and only Trixie is dependent upon a man. Alma, with her brief exercise of true capitalist power, loses the most: still wealthy but no longer in control of her claim, the two husbands she married for convenience murdered, and the man she loves passionately forever out of reach. Yet the one woman who never seeks to exceed her place, Martha Bullock, suffers the loss of both a husband and a son, making it difficult to read Alma's ill fortune purely as punishment for her hubris in daring to strive for equal status in a man's world.

Still, the narrative does require that the others become more like Martha's conventional helpmate. Indeed, she forms a nexus that encompasses them all. Trixie is the lover of Martha's husband's best friend and partner and works in his store. Jane and Joanie assist Martha in the school where Martha teaches Alma's adopted daughter, Sofia. For her part, Martha is compassionate, resilient, and no doormat. Nevertheless she constrains her own desires to what is possible under patriarchy and tempers her hurt at her husband's affair with Alma through polite indirection in her conversations with his former mistress and forgiveness of his betrayal: "That poor woman. Husband killed, left alone. Any person would have found her situation sympathetic, let alone someone of your instincts" (2.8). Once again, *Deadwood* valorizes the woman who stands by the man who has done her wrong. As for women who think they can defeat men at their own game, the viewer can only look to the fate of Maddie, Joanie's partner in the Chez Ami. "She wasn't scared of any man—the first I ever met," Joanie tells Charlie. "My Momma feared my Daddy and I did and my sisters too. I never met a girl till Maddie that wasn't afraid of men"—to which Charlie replies, "And Maddie's dead now?" (2.7). That says it all.

87

The women who survive in *Deadwood* ultimately seem to do so because they possess the "natural" female impulse to nurture children. Millichap notes how "they all flock together, reputable and disreputable, in protection of the orphaned Sofia Metz" (109). Paradoxically, though, this emphasis on mothering exists within a context that sees a functioning nuclear family as doomed. Sofia's biological family dies on the road as they leave the camp, and Pinkertons kill her beloved foster father, Ellsworth. Martha and Seth Bullock lose William. Odell, the estranged son of Lou Marchbanks, the woman whom Hearst brings in to cook after he purchases the Grand Central, also perishes. While some of the children who attend the school must have both mothers and fathers at home, the viewer never sees them. As for what the viewer knows of the adult characters' backgrounds, oppressive fathers are the norm, perhaps as a reflection of Milch's own upbringing. Sol Star, whom Trixie regards as too "healthy-minded" to grasp all the depravity that goes on in Deadwood, is an exception in that he quotes with respect many sayings of his late father.

Yet even Sol makes no mention of his mother. On the few occasions when characters do speak of their mothers, it is not to praise them. If fathers abuse, mothers abandon, either by leaving or dying. Most egregious in this regard is Al Swearengen's mother. She drops him off at the brutal orphanage run by the monstrous mother-figure and pimp "Mrs. fat ass fuckin' Anderson" in order to work as a whore in Georgia. All these years later, she dominates his fantasies and serves as a central topic of his fellatio monologues. Like the man himself, she is an ambivalent figure. On the one hand, he imagines she became an (unlikely) "mayor or some other type of success story"; on the other, she may have been degraded to a mere "ditch for fucking come" (1.11 "Jewel's Boot Is Made for Walking"). Given Al's admiration for the intrepid and ruthless undercover Pinkerton agent Miss Isringhausen, he may have justified his mother freeing herself of him if it led to independence and success. In other words, he credits her alternately with being an excellent role model whose ruthless pragmatism he has emulated to secure his own success and a worthless, debased abdicator of her sacred maternal duty who deserves to be treated as he treats the women who work for him at the Gem. In a second fantasy, Al recalls his conviction as a boy that she had changed her mind and wanted him back, if only the orphanage proctor had not held him down to prevent his running to her: "Christ, I'd have wished to—though probably she'd have thrown me overboard anyway—but I'd have wished to get to that fucking ship" (3.4 "Full Faith and Credit"). Al likes to think of himself as someone who wouldn't hesitate to toss an inconvenient offspring overboard, but, just as he still wishes he could have made it onto the ship, he still slips on occasion and gives in to compassion. Perhaps this is what Milch is trying to explain when he speaks of Swearengen both exploiting and rescuing his whores. The conflicted view of his mother certainly resonates in his love for Trixie, who embodies both versions of her simultaneously, giving their relationship an incestuous inflection.

What might have happened had Al's mother clung to him? Could the presence and primacy in a child's life of a devoted mother have made any difference for the wounded and destructive individuals who dominate the *Deadwood* dramatis personae? The character of Richardson provides some evidence that the answer may be "yes." Richardson—mentally challenged, with rotten teeth, a bald pate, but a scraggly gray beard and a long fringe of hair where hair grows at all—is in Farnum's employ as the cook for the Grand Central's guests. Finding in him at least one person to whom he can feel superior, Farnum constantly berates Richardson and sometimes kicks and slaps him. Indeed, he projects onto this hapless employee many of the failings others see in him. Thus, if Hearst can refer to E. B. as someone who "looks like he stepped out of a specimen box," Farnum will consistently speak of Richardson as if he were not quite human. He "imagine[s] you foraging for berries and grubs, and flicking at insects with your sticky tongue" (3.3), asks "could you have been born, Richardson, and not egg-hatched as I've always assumed?" (3.2) and, even when rehearsing an insincere profession of loyalty to his beleaguered employee as an excuse for not wanting to sell the hotel, compares him to "a beloved household pet" (2.5). Yet Richardson is completely loyal to his tormentor, nursing Farnum when he has suffered a beating and saving his life when he chokes on a poultice for a toothache, both of which acts of kindness Farnum treats with typical ingratitude.

The viewer can hardly imagine how a man with Richardson's limitations has survived on his own in the rough-and-ready frontier or how he came to the camp. Only two facts about his background are revealed: "my father didn't like me" and "I loved my mother." That he had a disapproving father is consistent with *Deadwood*'s overall themes, but the fact that he apparently had a present mother whom he loved is unique for the adult characters. Farnum's startling retort, "puberty may bring you to understand what we take for mother love is re-

89

ally murderous hatred and a desire for revenge" (3.2) jibes with Swearengen's attitude and perhaps gives viewers a clue as to why so many men on the series are content to debase and exploit women.

Richardson's positive maternal relationship, on the other hand, creates in him a reverence for women. Alma, though somewhat uneasy around him, especially when he says "I like you. You're pretty" (2.5), asks him to perform small errands for her and chooses him to escort her to the Gem and go in to inquire for Trixie. While she waits, she absentmindedly picks up a pair of bleached antlers from a box near the entrance and then gives them to Richardson to dispose of when he returns. But Richardson retains them as a precious token from the lady he worships from afar. He goes on, apparently, to create his own religion around them, periodically lifting them in supplication to the giant, horned deer head mounted above the hotel's staircase. One might say that these prayers work, because he later receives an even better gift—a new mother in the form of "Aunt" Lou. While she displaces Richardson from his job, she

Richardson beseeches his antler god to keep his loved ones safe. (Also pictured is Claudia, one of the actors in Langrishe's theatrical troupe.)

takes him on as her assistant, teaching him how to maximize his mental abilities in order to work more efficiently, calls him her "lucky charm," dresses him up in a suit, and coaches him on how to vote on election day.

Richardson's antler religion looks like some sort of phallic compensation, as if he were seeking repair of his impaired masculinity so as to function better within Deadwood's violent regime. This is how Swearengen reads it, saying, "Tell your god to ready for blood," as he passes the supplicant with antler raised. But when the actress Claudia asks him the meaning of his devotions, he replies, "Praying for my loved ones." A definitive rebuttal to his tormentor Farnum's view of the nature of maternal affections, and perhaps confirmation of woman's true power as *Deadwood* conceives of it, Richardson's mother's unlovely son radiates pure love.

91

Dirt Worshippers and Celestials and Niggers . . . Oh, My!

Right to vote shall not be abridged or
denied on account of race or color or
condition of previous servitude. Fifteenth
Amendment to the U.S. Constitution,
ratified 1870, law of the land thereafter,
including territories.

*Rutherford, resident cynic of the No. 10
saloon*

Perhaps as shocking as hearing the words *cocksucker, fuck,*
and *cunt* thrown around so casually on *Deadwood* is hearing the racial epithets *chink, coon,* and *nigger,* as well as blatant
bigotry voiced with no attempt at self-censorship. Even though
expressions of overt racism are much more historically accurate than men saying *fuck* and its variants as the adjective and
adverb of choice within every utterance, twenty-first-century
television is much more wary of the former than the latter. But
purging the Western of hate speech would, to Milch, be just as
disingenuous as using all those euphemisms like "goldurned"
that used to pass for swearing in the classic model of the genre.

The camp reproduces the racial and ethnic diversity that
distinguished America from the more homogenous populations

of Old World nations and the simultaneous emergence of a vocabulary and a politics that sought to make each an enemy to each. In the first episode alone, Swearengen is a "limey" whom Irish Tim Driscoll believes will try to cheat him as his ancestors always have. The Metz family are Scandinavians, known as "squareheads" locally. More politely, Reverend Smith receives with pleasure the knowledge that Star was born in Vienna, Austria, and Bullock in Ontario, Canada; but back in Montana the lynch mob expresses contempt when Sol comes to Seth's aid, for who is going to fear "a Jew on a wagon"? And Indians, falsely accused of massacring the Metzes, are "bloodthirsty," "heathen," and "savages."

Eschewing any sentimental view of an American melting pot, *Deadwood* nevertheless also presents instances in which the community can transcend racial and ethnic divisions, much as friendships and alliances form between criminal and lawman or whore and Victorian lady. To a certain extent the show oversimplifies the pervasiveness of racism at such a time and in such a setting. The hooples, Pinkertons, and pimps spew hate speech, but the more educated, noncriminal element to a person treat all ethnicities equally and with irreproachable politeness, just as they invariably treat whores like ladies. Bullock has a Jew for a business partner. He is able to empathize with the Sioux who attacked him and regrets having to kill him. He declares to another lynch mob, "People angry at their difficulties often act like fuckin' idiots, but there'll be no murdering people in this camp of any color" (2.6). Even the rough-hewn Jane, by virtue of her membership in the Bullock-Hickok nexus, has no qualms about sharing a bottle with an African American: "Don't fuckin' look around! I don't care who sees a nigger drinkin' with me or drinkin' from the same bottle or how . . . stupid his fucking outfit is" (2.5). To be sure, some hooples may surprise, as when the sardonic Rutherford leaves the No. 10 to escort the self-proclaimed "Nigger General" Fields to the polls, quoting the Fifteenth Amendment to those who would try to deny him suffrage. Swearengen, of course, occupies a middle ground. He has a racial slur for every occasion but also will work with anyone, regardless of race, creed, or color, if that individual shares a common objective.

Bigotry becomes one factor in creating violent confrontation and limiting access to economic self-interest, but those who are not white Christians sometimes can and do find a place to prosper in the camp: "Discrimination, based on level of sobriety, gender identity, race, even language ability, certainly occurs in *Deadwood,* yet entrepreneurial individualism can erode social hierarchies" (Worden 234). In examining the economic fortunes of four ethnic groups prominent in the *Deadwood* narrative—Jews, Chinese, Native Americans, and African Americans—viewers will observe successful individuals outside of white Christian manhood, but there are certainly no guarantees. Such stories of minority success also illuminate further the natures of the dominant majority with whom they are inextricably joined in the emergence of the community so central to the show.

The Jew

Sol Star is the only series regular who belongs to a minority, and he is the only one of his ethnicity featured in the camp. Being Jewish does not seem to have any negative impact on his ability to achieve financial success and gain respect in the community. The hardware store prospers, and he is chief officer in the Bank of Deadwood. Despite a blatantly anti-Semitic stump speech by his opponent, Farnum, Star wins the mayoral election handily. Yet it is not as if his Jewishness simply vanishes from popular perception. Others refer to him as "the Jew" seemingly more often than as Sol or Mr. Star. Even Trixie, his lover, calls him "the Jew" in third-party conversations, although often affectionately as "my Jew." And when they have disagreements, she attributes them frequently to his Jewish characteristics.

The most direct anti-Semitism he faces comes from Swearengen. When Star and Bullock first negotiate to purchase the lot they are renting, Al interrupts Sol's attempt to mediate between Bullock and Swearengen with "Why don't you do whatever you people do when you're not running your mouths off or cheatin' people out of what they earn by Christian work?"(1.2 "Deep Water"). Bullock later expresses surprise that Sol took this in stride, but his partner notes that he's had "worse from better." Eventually, though, he does tell Swearengen to stop the insults if he expects his cooperation in the scheme to fabricate Montana's interest in annexing the camp. By this time, their relationship has been complicated by the fact of Al's bedmate Trixie leaving Al to cohabit with Star. Initially outraged, Swearengen comes around and supports the couple, even arranging to put Star in a house that shares a wall with Trixie's lodgings, so that they can keep their relationship from becoming too public as Star seeks to become mayor, a position perhaps not compatible with openly having a former whore as a lover. None of this support stops Al from making his anti-Semitic remarks, however, any more than the loyalty he feels for his Gem "family" stops him from abusing them verbally.

The primary canard that Swearengen levels against Jews is that they are obsessed with making money. In one of their first conversations, Al notes that Star is a Jewish name and follows up with "marked you for an earner the minute you come in my sight"—and mutters "Jew bastard" the minute he is out of it. Even if this were not a misrepresentation of a whole people, one rooted in centuries of stereotypes of avaricious moneylenders, it does seem disingenuous coming from Al in this particular time and place, since Deadwood exists to attract people who are obsessed with striking it rich. Whatever disdain Swearengen feels about Star's ethnicity nevertheless does not stop him from including him in every meeting he calls of the movers and shakers in the camp. Indeed, Star and Swearengen have a lot in common in regard to their business acumen and administrative

Sol and Trixie enjoy a quiet, post-coital moment in their tumultuous relationship.

savvy; it's no surprise that Trixie, also an able strategic thinker when not in the thrall of her mercurial temper, should have been attracted to both of them. At one point Al counsels her to demand payment for sexual services because no Jew would respect anyone who gave away something of value without charging for it. When Trixie replies that she is not being paid but that Sol is teaching her bookkeeping, his reply reveals that he has a more nuanced view of Jewish culture than he usually lets on: "That's all right then. Learnin' is like currency to them" (2.6).

The Chinese

Keone Young, who plays Mr. Wu, should have had some serious discussions with his agent for not getting him regular billing over the likes of the child actors who played Sofia and William. As previous chapters have revealed, Wu's character arc is far more central to the overall themes and plot of *Deadwood* than is Sol Star's. At least Milch gives him his own chapter in *Deadwood: Stories of the Black Hills*. Beyond Wu's own rise to "big man" status, he is the leader of a whole community of Chinese who play an integral part in the workings of the camp and have their own demarcated area, "Chink Alley," within it. The Chinese are the only non-white, non-Christian racial group present in substantial numbers throughout the series. They tend to do the "dirty work" of the camp: laundry, butchering meat, unofficial corpse disposal, as well as purveying the vices that the saloon and brothel owners do. Paul Wright and Hailin Zhou observe that the Chinese become "both a rival to and a microcosm of the political landscape of the town at large"; they "are seen not only in the light of their all-too-real victimization, but also in the shadow of their collaboration with the darker genius of the American frontier spirit" (158).

While Swearengen makes common cause with his potential rival, Wu, Tolliver seeks to usurp Chinese hegemony over their own businesses just as he tries to poach all the best customers from the Gem. He buys up land in the Chinese district and partners in the marketing of the brutally treated Chinese prostitutes, telling his shills to stress their exotic "snatch," which can supposedly rival the grip of a python. For this reason, perhaps, anti-Chinese rhetoric issues more from the Bella Union crowd than from any other quarter. Leon's remark to Wu that "You may be a big shot in this alley but you are less than a nigger to me" (1.12) emblemizes this attitude. Wu's pidgin English and voluble gesticulations sometimes render his portrayal close to a racist stereotype, but such stereotypes, however discomfiting, pale beside murderous hatred like that which Leon expresses.

The downside for the Chinese in *Deadwood* lies in the fact of their willingness to work hard in deplorable conditions. Hearst gradually displaces not only the prospectors who first developed the claims but also the German and Cornish immigrant mine workers with Chinese laborers as part of a "dehumanizing project to undermine labor standards, earning power, and entrepreneurial confidence in the camp's existing arrangements" (Wright and Zhou 164). Such concerns, which began in California, eventually led to the Chinese Exclusion Act of 1882, and free Chinese immigration to the United States did not begin again until 1943. Nevertheless, to a twenty-first-century audience, Chinese economic success does not seem any more unusual than Jewish success. That Wu and Star conform to the neoliberal paradigm as they prosper also means that their stories become subsumed into the larger economic narrative of the show. On the other hand, the success narrative for Native Americans and African Americans in the aggregate does not look so rosy 130 years later; perhaps this explains why *Deadwood* does not portray an Indian Wu or a black Star.

Native Americans

Indians do not appear as individualized, present characters in *Deadwood*. Neither the vicious villains of many classic Westerns nor the noble children of nature of many revisionist ones, they are simply the already displaced first losers in the economic narrative of the nation and the camp, their Pyrrhic victory against Custer notwithstanding. The abrogation of the Fort Laramie Treaty signifies that an America that contains within its borders sovereign, self-determined Indian nations that operate according to a more material economy than "the symbolic logic of gold" is an impossibility. "Taking the gold from the Indians is our original sin," Milch writes. "That's what comes before. *Deadwood* is the story of what comes after" (53). Thus viewers only hear conversations about the Sioux and the Cheyenne as the army hunts them down and forces them to accept life on reservations where corrupt Indian agents rob them blind. Remarks from General Crook's soldiers indicate a deep hatred for their enemy and hint at revengeful atrocities against them. When murdered camp residents disappear in Wu's pigpen, supposed death at Indian hands is a popular alibi for the cover-up. But because he did not want to exempt his characters from any responsibility for this sin, Milch does include one story arc featuring Native Americans present on-screen.

When news of the massacre of the Metzes reaches the camp, it looks like all the evening's customers at the Gem may charge out to look for the Indians upon whom Persimmon Phil and his gang try to pin the blame. To lessen the adverse effects on his business, Al offers a free drink and, for those who wait to ride out after dawn, "a personal $50 bounty for every decapitated head of as many of these godless heathen cocksuckers as anyone can bring in" (1.1). Only one person claims the bounty, a Mexican who rides into camp brandishing such a head above him. (Mexicans, another staple of the traditional Western, have their only representation here, which is somewhat plausible considering how far north of the border the Black Hills are.) As fate (and *Deadwood* thematics) would have it, the Sioux who attacks Bullock is in the process of performing funeral rites for this very same Native American, "his headless buddy." As Charlie explains, "that's what you nearly got killed for. Interfering with his big fuckin' medicine, burying his fuckin' buddy, over the fuckin' ridge!" (1.6). The scar Bullock carries on his forehead from this encounter becomes a mark of Cain, a reminder that when original sin expels humans from Eden, the next generation grounds its social relations in violence.

Meanwhile, as discussed previously, the decapitated head remains in Al's custody. He neither disposes of it nor displays it as a curiosity but projects an identity onto it and then uses it as an interlocutor, particularly concerning his growing fears that he also may end up dispossessed of his holdings. Perplexed by Hearst's drive for utter control of the camp, Al asks, "Watching us advance on your stupid teepee, Chief, knowing you had to make your move . . . did you not just want first to fucking understand?" (3.5 "A Two-Headed Beast"). When Swearengen wonders if he has been shortsighted in not learning how to handle a gun as the utility of close-contact throat slitting wanes, he warns Chief not to "say" anything: "And you ain't exactly the one to be leveling criticisms on the score of being slow to adapt. You fucking people are the original slow fucking learners!" (3.12).

Thus, despite often expressed verbal disdain for "dirt worshippers" and with no compunction about scapegoating them for his own ends, Swearengen grasps full well that Native Americans have not been robbed and slaughtered by whites for any but economic reasons; divine retribution for their sins or divine sanction to their despoilers does not enter into the money equation in *Deadwood*. Al states this outright in an exchange with Merrick:

> Merrick: Which is to say the economic motive is but one strand in the social tapestry my exemplary account would weave.
> Al: Ass-fucking the dirt worshippers being another, huh, as a pleasure beyond gain?
> . . . .
> Merrick: A more elevated perspective would construe our conduct as white men to be enacting a Manifest Destiny.
> Al: Whereas the warp, woof and fucking weave of my story's tapestry would foster the illusions of further commerce, huh? (2.2)

African Americans

If genocide against the indigenous population is the nation's original sin, then the importation of African slaves is the second. After the Civil War many emancipated blacks did try to start over in the West, a fact ignored for many years in films and television programs of the genre. *Deadwood* portrays four African Americans in two separate story arcs. Lou Marchbanks serves as George Hearst's cook, much as she did in the days when she was his slave. She has sent her son Odell to be raised in Liberia, but he returns, having discovered gold there and eager to partner with Hearst in mining it. Livery owner Hostetler has prospered in the camp as a businessman and is less than pleased when his outspoken friend, the "Nigger General" Fields, arrives. Although Lou has several scenes with Fields, their stories do not fundamentally intersect but rather proceed on parallel thematic lines. In both cases tragedy strikes and is tangentially, if not directly, linked to white racism. Nevertheless, the survivor of the pair forms a bond with a white man, although these cross-racial relationships are tinged with irony.

Lou expertly plays the part of the faithful house slave, subservient and eager to please her former master. She fusses about his welfare, cleans his boots, and takes over kitchen duties when he acquires the Grand Central Hotel. Hearst affects racial tolerance by insisting that she have a room in the hotel, but this is more a way in which he exercises his will than any belief in black equality. Out of his presence, Lou is a completely different person, contemptuous of his hypocrisy. Viewers see her in "Chink Alley" on the night after her arrival boisterously beating the Chinese at their own game (mah-jongg), drinking, smoking a cigar, and demonstrating knowledge of their language. And because they don't reciprocally understand English, she takes the opportunity to express her real feelings toward Hearst:

> "I love your cobbler like sunset, Lou." And back-broke niggers in the fields. George Hearst . . . he do love his nose in a hole more, and ass in the air, and back legs kickin' out little lumps of gold like a fucking badger. No more use for them nuggets, either. Past counting them up, and saying that big number to astonish niggers to remind us we in the world. (3.3)

Lou never explains why she would continue to bow and scrape to Hearst, given her abilities, but viewers see what happens to anyone who defies his will. She does express a prescient fear that the Reconstruction-era opportunities available to African Americans won't last, as evidenced by her sending Odell to Liberia "so the hell that was coming here for niggers wouldn't burn you up" (3.7 "Unauthorized Cinnamon"). Her anxiety proves well founded when Odell is murdered on his way to meet with a Hearst agent in New York; that Hearst has eliminated the middleman between himself and the Liberian gold seems highly likely, even if Odell is the son of his supposedly beloved retainer and despite Hearst's proclamation that possession of the color could make a man *of color* the equal to a white man. These events give Richardson a chance to repay all of Lou's kindnesses to him as the viewer sees him comforting her when news of her son's death arrives.

The tragicomic saga of Steve the drunk, Hostetler, and the Nigger General Fields winds its way through two seasons of the show and embroils Star and Bullock as well. (It is notable that Swearengen, who has his fingers in every Deadwood pie, never becomes involved in the story arcs of any of the African American characters.) In a way Hostetler and Fields mirror the two hardware store owners. Fields, like Star, accepts that he will have to deal with bigotry and gets along as best as his wits can carry him without stopping to internalize the insults that come his way. Hostetler, on the other hand, barely controls his rage. It threatens to boil over at any minute and lead to violence. The only reason he doesn't give into it as often as Bullock does is because he fears the consequences for any black man who does so. This fear constantly wars with his pride and makes him ashamed when he acts according to the dictates of self-preservation rather than principle.

Viewers first meet Hostetler as the owner of the thriving camp livery stable, a man who has done well enough that he has a second parcel of land to sell, which Bullock buys from him with plans to build a house. The arrival of Fields just as the camp has to deal with the uncertainty about the status of claims begins a chain of events that destroys him and his prosperity.

Steve, the inebriated instigator of racial violence against African Americans, represents *Deadwood*'s sustained analysis of the economic roots of racism, an analysis that resonates just as strongly in the post–Civil Rights Era. Although he holds traditionally racist views about African American inferiority, frequently referring to them as "monkeys," "lemurs," and less than human, his hatred springs from the belief that working-class whites must compete for economic success with blacks and that blacks have been favored by those whites with political and financial clout. Farnum also expresses this view when he opines that Richardson has been replaced as the Grand Central's cook not because he is "a grotesque of inconceivable stupidity" but because he is not a "repulsively obese" black woman (3.3).

Perpetually inebriated, Steve is the archetypal hoople-head. In a trenchant commentary, Al defines these men as drunk, stupid, and looking for anyone or anything to blame rather than accept that the causes of their failures lie with themselves (2.5). Upon learning that his claim may be forfeit, Steve first leads a mob against Jarry. When Bullock intervenes, he turns his discontent toward the newly arrived Fields. In the grip of addled reasoning, Steve blames blacks for losing his chance to inherit the family confectionery business because he was drafted into the Union Army. Bullock once again prevents Steve from carrying out his violent ends but not before Steve has tarred Fields' shoulder. Hostetler had hidden Fields but gave him up when the mob burst into the livery. Even though Fields completely forgives him, saying he would have done the same thing, only quicker, Hostetler cannot forgive himself.

The first act of the tragedy culminates the next day when Bullock, agitated by thoughts of Alma, accosts Steve at the No. 10 to impress upon him that he will not tolerate mob violence. Not liking Steve's attitude, he punches him in the face. Egged on by the troublemaker Rutherford, Steve vows in recompense to sodomize Bullock's horse and carve upon its hindquarters what he has done. In the event, he merely masturbates on its leg but is caught in the act at the livery by Hostetler and Fields. Hostetler is ready to kill Steve, but Fields pulls him back from this irrevocable action, getting the drunk instead to write on a slate "I fucked Bullock's horse," with the stipulation that said declaration be held for blackmail purposes should Steve ever trouble them again.

Fate will not preserve this uneasy truce, however. When a wild horse escapes at the livery, it breaks Steve's leg and tramples William Bullock to death, and Hostetler and Fields panic and run, leaving the animals in their charge unattended. For once Steve proves useful, stepping in to see to their care and run the livery, a reversal of his attempt to violate and maim the sheriff's horse. That horses are at the center of the economic conflict that ensues when Hostetler returns marks still another way in which the show subordinates the myth of the West to the operations of "Amalgamation and Capital," the title of the episode in which the wild horse goes on its rampage. (For a political take on this incident, see Wiggins and Holmberg.)

To Steve, the black man's legal title to the livery as opposed to his own sweat equity recapitulates Yankton's threatened in-

Hostetler and the "Nigger General" Fields find Steve the drunk assaulting a horse and order him to sign a document stating his offense.

validation of the mining claims. He furthermore sees the possibility of losing his newfound economic security as a continuation both of his own personal bad luck, starting back in his native Utica, New York, and that of his family, who have never been able to hold onto any wealth. For a while, however, it looks as though the cycle may be broken. Bullock and Star broker an elaborate plan for Hostetler to sell the livery to Steve, financed by a loan from the Bank of Deadwood, and leave the camp for a fresh start in Oregon. The foolish pride and race hatreds that animate both men constantly threaten to derail the deal—there has to be a simultaneous signing of the contracts so that neither will be seen to surrender first—but at last it is done, and the often comic struggles look to have a happy ending. But Steve cannot leave good luck alone and demands that the incriminating slate be turned over to him, then becomes uncertain whether the one produced is the actual slate that he signed. Hostetler, infuriated, strides into another part of the barn and blows his head off, whether intentionally or accidentally is never determined. And still Steve cannot refrain from snatching defeat from the jaws of victory. He has no head for accounts (especially when in his favored drunken state) and wants Fields to stay and help him run the business, even while hurling racist taunts at him and swearing that he will never put their two names together on the livery's signage. As a last-ditch effort to force the Nigger General not to depart, he decides to remove one of his horse's shoes. The next time the episode returns to Steve, he is lying insensible in the straw, a kick in the head from the horse having damaged him so severely that he lacks all higher cognitive functions.

Having established the destructive effect of racism on those whom it consumes, *Deadwood* offers an ironic and (perhaps) hopeful coda. Although Fields had intended an immediate departure for San Francisco, after first taking some *schadenfreude* in Steve's all too condign punishment, he begins to look after him. He hauls him around the camp in a wheelbarrow and, when that isn't practical, pays Steve's old cronies at the No. 10 to take care of him. The last the viewer sees of the two, they are at the polls, where Fields casts his vote despite efforts by the Pinkertons to block him.

The writers may intend for viewers to read this as an act of Christian forgiveness on Fields' part, and it plays as very moving. Of course, such a reading begs the question of why it is the African American who needs to do the forgiving; had the positions been reversed, Steve likely would not have done the same. *Deadwood* does tend to use women and minorities as exemplars of redemption for its large, flawed white male cast of characters rather than investing in them as people in their own right. The only white men with whom blacks can form a close bond are, after all, a mentally challenged individual (Richardson) and someone in a persistent vegetative state (Steve). A more subtle and evenhanded expression of the futility of seeing difference rather than common humanity between blacks and whites occurs when Steve and Fields sign documents at the bank, for it is revealed that Steve the drunk's surname is also Fields and that the Nigger General's first name is Samuel. So, had Steve written "S. Fields Livery" on his sign, he would have included the black man as an equal simply by representing himself.

There's a bloodstain on your floor.
Seth Bullock

A month before *Deadwood*'s third season premiered on June 11, 2006, media reports confirmed that there would not be a fourth. Milch had developed a new show for HBO, *John from Cincinnati,* and network president Chris Albrecht did not believe that Milch, given his singular work habits, could launch it the next year while also trying to produce twelve episodes of *Deadwood.* The average $4.5–$5 million per episode price tag probably also contributed to the network's desire for a shorter fourth season. Albrecht offered a six-episode commitment but Milch declined. When *Deadwood* viewers protested in significant numbers, the two negotiated a compromise. Milch would instead produce 2 two-hour movies that covered a longer amount of narrative time per hour than usual and would bring the series to a definite conclusion. An appropriate end point might have been the 1879 fire that destroyed most of the town. Harry Manning and Tom Nuttall's acquisition of a fire engine and Milch's remarks to the *New York Times* about covering actual historical events, "including perhaps a fire and a flood" (McKinley, A1) point in this direction.

Deadwood viewers will never know, however. The two movies did not materialize, in part due to Albrecht losing his job at HBO when he was charged in 2007 with assaulting his girlfriend. Meanwhile, Milch's new show premiered almost a year to the day after *Deadwood*'s third season began. *John from Cincinnati,* a fuzzy allegory in which a heavenly visitor announces that the Second Coming and a post-9/11 apocalypse will play out through three generations of a family of California surfers, was a colossal failure; it did not receive renewal after its 10-episode run. In light of this, HBO's desire to keep Milch happy had waned. Albrecht had said that his motivation to offer the *Deadwood* wrap-up movies came from a fear that "the real victim would be 'John from Cincinnati,' because it would be 'The Show They Canceled "Deadwood" For'" (McKinley A36). As events played out, fans changed the formulation slightly to "*This* Is the Show They Canceled 'Deadwood' For?!?"

Thus, the inconclusive ending of season three is the ending that remains. It's not the cliff-hanger that some canceled series leave their viewers to ponder but rather a snapshot of people slowly stepping back from the edge of the precipice yet not quite out of danger of falling. Critics have different views on just how complete Hearst's triumph is. Salerno sees it as circumscribed by the contrasting pull of the resistant community: "Even those in power can act only to the extent that the public allows them to: the strongest autocrat can be deposed when indignities become intolerable enough to overcome fear" (208). Mark L. Berettini, on the other hand, believes that Hearst has been able to "annihilate" the camp's endeavors "in favor of his own interests and of the State." And he sees this process not as the end but as a harbinger of more oppressive restriction to come: "If Hearst is a murderous engine, then as such, he is just the beginning of the train" (262). Worden, as discussed in Chapter Four, sees the neoliberal economics of the camp's inhabitants as generating a means to undo free-market brutality from the inside; Kyle Wiggins and David Holmberg are much more pessimistic, saying that, through Hearst, "the unmitigated violence that secured Deadwood as a stolen gold farm is precisely the mechanism that destroys the camp's mastery" (294).

My own evaluation of where *Deadwood* leaves viewers concentrates on the image with which it concludes: Al Swearengen, on his knees, scrubbing the floor of the bloodstain left when he slit Jen's throat. The bloodstained floor is a trope that runs throughout the series. It signifies the foundational violence informing not only the camp but all of American history; whether in 1776, 1876, or 2006, whether to preserve its citizens' liberties or aid in their acquisitive despoliations, it remains. There is no glorious march of civilization forward to relegate the series' events to a distant past. Like the "damned spot" on Lady Macbeth's hands, it can never completely vanish no matter how hard one scrubs.

One room at the Grand Central Hotel becomes a permanently low-rent lodging because of the residue from Tim Driscoll's murder. The Gem, in particular, is a site of such regular bloodshed that bringing out the bucket and brush takes on almost ritualistic significance, like the serving of peaches at town meetings. Probably the most important previous scene involving the bloodstain on the floor occurs when Bullock agrees to become sheriff while standing opposite Swearengen in the very office in which Magistrate Claggett had his throat cut only hours before. By noting the stain but not moving to interrogate Al about its origins, Bullock tacitly consents to look the other way in order for the goals that he and Swearengen share to be realized. Al concludes their meeting with the valedictory, "Anyways, Sheriff, I'm gonna walk past that bloodstain that mysteriously appeared and go oversee my business interests. Take your time" (1.12).

Although Jen's death in season 3 also serves to preserve Deadwood as a community more favorable to Swearengen's

111

business interests, it is fundamentally different from the murders that have preceded it. Everyone else on Al's hit list "had it coming" in some way. Most are criminals or corrupt power brokers; at the very least they have overtly threatened him. But Jen is innocent. Sacrificing her still has utilitarian value but lacks any moral justification, even under as contingent a moral code as Swearengen's. He articulates his misgivings to the Chief, dreading the many days that he will have to endure the other whores chastising him: "'Ooh, how could you? How could you?' With their big fucking cow eyes." He continues, "What's the fucking alternative? I ain't fuckin' killing *her* that sat nights with me sick and taking slaps to her mug that were some less than fucking fair" (3.12 "Tell Him Something Pretty"). This implicates the audience in Jen's death as well, for as much as viewers may bridle at her undeserved fate, especially through identification with Johnny's love for her, they "know" Trixie much better. After the shock of three-season regular Ellsworth's slaying, they too are likely to accept the substitution, rather than see Trixie die as well.

Earlier Dan had offered to send Jewel up to deal with the stain, but Al says it must remain until the ruse is perpetrated, "and when that's over, if we're still alive, I'll clean my own fucking mess up." This is the only answer that *Deadwood* offers to the endemic violence in the American character: admit responsibility and clean up after yourself as best you can. (When Tolliver, ever Swearengen's dark mirror, brags to Joanie about how he cleaned up the gore of her murdered friends at the Chez Ami to spare her, she replies skeptically: "Don't tell me you cleaned up anyone's gore, Cy.") The last shot of the series shows Swearengen humbled, in long shot and from a high angle, with his head cast down as he continues to scrub, a marked difference from the usual frame-dominating close-ups and low angled shots lavished upon him. He thus fulfills Milch's ultimate description of an American: "He makes do with what's in front

112

Al cleans the blood of the murdered prostitute Jen off the floor in the show's final image.

of him. He takes things the way they are and doesn't pretend they're something else" (213).

Deadwood viewers may be left in doubt as to the futures of its large cast of characters but can make do nicely with the moments of surprising connection or revelation that surface at unexpected moments. Wu offers tea to Jewel, shivering in the cold as she stands vigil outside Doc Cochran's, where William lies dying. Fields brings Steve to amateur night in his wheelbarrow, lifts a bottle of whiskey and says, "Isn't this fun, man?" During that same event, "imbecile" Richardson astonishes all with his proficiency as a juggler. A tree grows as if by magic inside a schoolhouse guarded by the giant Mose Manuel. Martha Bullock asks her husband to promise that no harm will come to the horse that trampled her child to death. Given Milch's metaphor of the community as the body of Christ, I think we can call these instances moments of grace—and accept them with a *Deadwood* locution fallen out of fashion these days: "Huzzah!"

WORKS CITED

Akass, Kim. "You Motherfucker: Al Swearengen's Oedipal Dilemma." In **115** *Reading* Deadwood: *A Western to Swear By,* ed. David Lavery. (London: I. B. Tauris, 2006), 23–32.

Benz, Brad. "Deadwood and the English Language." *Great Plains Quarterly.* 27.4 (2007): 239–51.

Berettini, Mark L. "No Law: *Deadwood* and the State." *Great Plains Quarterly.* 27.4 (2007): 253–65.

Brockway, Cristi H. *Deadwood: The Complete Transcripts.* http://turtlegirl76.com/deadwood/indexOLD.htm.

Drysdale, David. "'Laws and Every Other Damn Thing': Authority, Bad Faith and the Unlikely Success of *Deadwood.*" In *Reading* Deadwood: *A Western to Swear By,* ed. David Lavery. (London: I. B. Tauris, 2006), 133–44.

Havrilesky, Heather. "The Man Behind 'Deadwood.'" Salon.com (5 March 2005). http://dir.salon.com/ent/feature/2005/03/05/milch/index.html

Hill, Erin. "'What's Afflictin' You?': Corporeality, Body Crises, and the Body Politic in *Deadwood.*" In *Reading* Deadwood: *A Western to Swear By,* ed. David Lavery. (London: I. B. Tauris, 2006), 171–84.

Howard, Douglas L. "Why Wild Bill Hickok Had to Die." In *Reading* Deadwood: *A Western to Swear By,* ed. David Lavery. (London: I. B. Tauris, 2006), 43–56.

Jacobs, Jason. "Al Swearengen, Philosopher King." In *Reading* Deadwood: *A Western to Swear By,* ed. David Lavery. (London: I. B. Tauris, 2006), 11–22.

Klein, Amanda Ann. "'The Horse Doesn't Get a Credit': The Foregrounding of Generic Syntax in *Deadwood*'s Opening Credits." In *Reading Deadwood: A Western to Swear By*, ed. David Lavery. (London: I. B. Tauris, 2006), 93–100.

Lowry, Brian. "Deadwood." *Variety*, 11 March 2004. http://www.variety.com/review/VE1117923370.html?categoryid=32&cs=1&query=deadwood

McCabe, Janet, and Kim Akass. "It's Not TV, It's HBO's Original Programming: Producing Quality TV." In *It's Not TV: Watching HBO in the Post-television Era*, ed. Marc Leverette, Brian L. Ott, and Cara Louise Buckley. (New York: Routledge, 2008), 83–93.

Mcgee, Patrick. *From Shane to Kill Bill: Rethinking the Western*. Oxford: Blackwell, 2007.

McKinley, Jesse. "The Sun Rises, Again, in the West." *The New York Times*, 11 June 2006. A1, A36.

Milch, David. *Deadwood: Stories of the Black Hills*. New York: Melcher, 2006.

Miller, Toby. "Foreword: It's television. It's HBO." In *It's Not TV: Watching HBO in the Post-television Era*, ed. Marc Leverette, Brian L. Ott, and Cara Louise Buckley. (New York: Routledge, 2008), ix–xii.

Millichap, Joseph. "Robert Penn Warren, David Milch, and the Literary Contexts of *Deadwood*." In *Reading Deadwood: A Western to Swear By*, ed. David Lavery. (London: I. B. Tauris, 2006), 101–14.

O'Sullivan, Sean. "Old, New, Borrowed, Blue: *Deadwood* and Serial Fiction." In *Reading Deadwood: A Western to Swear By*, ed. David Lavery. (London: I. B. Tauris, 2006), 115–29.

Petersen, Anne Helen. "'Whores and Other Feminists': Recovering *Deadwood*'s Unlikely Feminisms." *Great Plains Quarterly*. 27.4 (2007): 267–282.

Poniewozik, James. "TV: So Wicked He's Good." *Time*, 20 February, 2005. http://www.time.com/time/magazine/article/0,9171,1029858,00.html

Salerno, Daniel. "'I Will Have You Bend': Language and the Discourses of Power in *Deadwood*." *Literary Imagination*. 12.2 (2010): 190–209.

Singer, Mark. "The Misfit: How David Milch Got from *NYPD Blue* to *Deadwood* by Way of an Epistle of St. Paul." *The New Yorker* (14 and 21 February 2005): 192–205.

Slotkin, Richard. *Gunfighter Nation*. Norman: University of Oklahoma Press, 1998.

Westerfelhaus, Robert, and Celeste Lacroix. "Waiting for the Barbarians: HBO's *Deadwood* as a Post-9/11 Ritual of Disquiet." *Southern Communications Journal* 74.1 (2009): 18–39.

Wiggins, Kyle, and David Holmberg. "'Gold is Every Man's Opportunity': Castration Anxiety and the Economic Venture in *Deadwood*." *Great Plains Quarterly.* 27.4 (2007): 283–95.

Worden, Daniel. "Neo-liberalism and the Western: HBO's *Deadwood* as National Allegory." *Canadian Review of American Studies,* 39.2 (2009): 222–46.

Wright, Paul and Hailin Zhou. "Divining the 'Celestials': The Chinese Subculture of *Deadwood*." In *Reading* Deadwood: *A Western to Swear By,* ed. David Lavery. (London: I. B. Tauris, 2006), 157–68.